The END TIMES Hoax and the Hijacking of Our Liberty

Steven and Debra Wallace

© 2010 Steven and Debra Wallace
All Rights Reserved.

No part of this publication may be reproduced, stored in a retrieval system, or transmitted, in any form or by any means, electronic, mechanical, photocopying, recording, or otherwise, without the written permission of the author.

First published by Dog Ear Publishing
4010 W. 86th Street, Ste H
Indianapolis, IN 46268
www.dogearpublishing.net

ISBN: 978-160844-379-6

This book is printed on acid-free paper.

Printed in the United States of America

Acknowledgements

This book is written with much gratitude to the ideas of:

Frederic Bastiat

Gary Craig

Andrew J. Galambos

G. Edward Griffin

Rose Wilder Lane

David Lipscomb

Richard Maybury

Thomas Paine

Ron Paul

Weston A. Price

Ayn Rand

Lew Rockwell

Jim Rogers

Butler Shaffer

Additionally, we are thankful for each other and the shared excitement and passion we both have for the subject matter. Co-authoring this book has been a deeply rewarding and life-enriching experience.

Dedication

This book is dedicated to the curious.

Table of Contents

Introduction 1

1. Why Questioning is Important 9
2. What is Truth? 15
   - *Is truth relative?* 16
   - *Does the truth need defending?* 18
3. Relationship of Truth to Belief 22
   - *What is the relationship between <u>fear</u> and our beliefs?* 24
4. The END TIMES Hoax 28
5. The END TIMES of the Judaic Age 42
6. What's Wrong with the Congregational Church Model? 78
7. Who Am I, What Am I Doing Here? 83
8. The Hijacking of Our Liberty 90

In Conclusion 110

Index 116

Introduction

This book is about liberty.

What are the liberty-limiting factors and beliefs that converge and contribute to the building and maintenance of the *institutional* structures (boxes or prisons) we each may find ourselves in?

What kind of mindset must we develop to empower ourselves to live a fulfilling life free from the *institutional* forces working together to break our spirit, destroy our dreams, and that leave us unwittingly resigned to live out our existence on earth within the boundaries set by other people and/or the *institutions* they seem to revere?

As we have always valued the ideas and honor of those stalwart souls who managed to walk straight paths unencumbered by the popular, but false, beliefs of their day and age, we also find joy in seeking out those ideas that are capable of withstanding intellectual scrutiny and that can be validated by reason.

Do truly sound ideas require those entertaining them to sever their minds from their bodies? Or, is it the other way around whereby, in actuality, it is the *unsound* ideas that require the intellectual decapitation of their victims?

We will share those exploratory questions we've asked in our quest for liberty with the hope of motivating others to continue the process.

Who can provide a convincing counter argument to the claim that most grief and human suffering, individually or collectively, have been the result of man not seeking and/or ignoring natural law in preference for an inferior, man-conceived, unjust, unequally applied, ever-changing, irresponsible, liberty-limiting, and centralized form of governance embracing political law, favors, graft, and corruption?

Is not the remedy to the human grief, suffering, and exploitation we see around us ultimately manifested in the abandonment of our dependency and subservience to an inferior, man-conceived form of governance?

Is not a form of governance whereby we voluntarily and individually adopt and embrace a more natural, superior, and liberating form of governance, in harmony with the laws of nature, a more humane and just societal existence?

Is not a form of governance that recognizes, in theory <u>and</u> practice, the equality of mankind, with each individual being granted autonomous freewill to be exercised within the framework of the golden rule, a much more superior form of governance?

Is not a form of governance that honors true equality also one that, quite naturally, expects individuals to be solely responsible for the consequences of their own decisions and actions?

Is not a form of governance whereby each individual is responsible for their own outcomes a much better form of governance than what we've recently witnessed with financial bailout after bailout of those who feel entitled to a free pass?

Can one honestly profess to believe in true equality while, at the same time, promote the creation of taxpayer-subsidized social safety nets for those who take risks and suffer losses?

Does natural law suggest that some men are more equal than others? Why would anyone endorse or give allegiance to any *institutional* authority or entity advocating, in theory or practice, equal opportunity to succeed while denying the same equal opportunity to fail? By what logic can those who take risks and succeed be expected to subsidize those who take risks and fail?

Is it not our duty and responsibility to free ourselves from the inequality promoting *institutions* shackling our minds and bodies so we can more easily recognize truth when we encounter it and, subsequently, apply those truths to a more liberated and empowered existence of our own design?

Were not the laws of nature instituted at the inception of the universe? Are not all the earth's inhabitants equally subject to the laws of nature?

It is important for us to share some of our biases and prejudices with the reader to foster a better understanding of our message. Understanding each other's models and how we each perceive the world around us is an important part of grasping why we each think and do the things we do.

After careful study, we have rejected our former belief in the divine right of kings, queens, principalities, and church authorities, etc., instilled in us from an early age and as former members of the church of Christ.

We unwittingly, but with the best of intentions, found ourselves operating increasingly within a system of man's design that did not make sense. We vainly and frustratingly attempted to mix our God-given reasoning abilities with our inherited faith.

Must we discard the ability to think and reason as a mechanism to retain our faith? Did not our Creator give us our ability to think and reason? Is not our ability to think and reason the filter for our faith? Conversely, is not the discarding of one's ability to think and reason the basis of a blind faith?

Does our Creator want us to be blind followers, or would he rather see us as purposeful and intense seekers of truth? For what reason would our Creator give us freewill if he expected blind faith and obedience? If blind faith is to be revered, why wouldn't our Creator have favored the creation of automatons instead of humans with the ability to think, reason, and choose?

How many of us even trust our own reasoning ability? How many of us have been conditioned by society to believe we need someone "wiser" to enlighten us to the truth? How many of us have abandoned our youthful idealism (when we still believed in our God-given reasoning ability) for the institutional *authoritarian* model? Can our ability to think and reason atrophy with non-use to the extent we lose our will to be free, or worse yet to not even understand what liberty is?

For ourselves, the only way we could retain our blind faith-based religious creed was to throw out our God-given ability to think and reason.

Who among us believes we are made in the image of God, from the standpoint of our minds and/or spirit? Who among us believes that our Creator would approve a dummying down, of sorts, of our ability to think and reason? Who among us believes to discard this gift of thinking and reasoning would be unpardonable, as our minds are the only thing significantly distinguishing mankind from the animal kingdom? How can we advocate throwing out our God-given ability to think and reason without advocating, at the same time, a blind faith, a blind obedience, and a blind unthinking god?

While our technological advances may have taken us to the moon, so to speak, have not our interactions with our fellow man, *institutionally* speaking, remained in a very primitive state of constant turmoil, strife, and war?

We knew there had to be a better way for mankind to interact with one another and did not believe the prevailing religious thought of the day that we need not concern ourselves about it because, "God is in control." While we agree that God is in control from the standpoint of the natural laws of the universe he designed to keep our planet from spinning out of control, we disagree vehemently that he "intervenes" in the affairs of man today by giving one king an advantage over another one. Was there not direct and observable evidence of "divine intervention" in days of old? Where is the evidence of such "divine intervention" today? Who benefits the most from those who continue to believe in the divine right of kings?

Who would tyrannical governments and evil regimes love the most, a compliant and sheep-like people waiting in their *institutional* holding pens to be "rescued," or individuals who accept personal responsibility for their condition and take action consistent with being personally responsible? Do tyrannical and evil governments promote individual responsibility and sovereignty or sheep-like dependency upon the State?

What is the intent of government when they falsely claim to protect us from terrorists, financial fraudsters, snake-oil salesmen, bad food and drugs, poverty, and illiteracy and with each point of failure insist that if only they had more money, more power, more personnel, and more regulations they could have protected us from, or prevented, those calamities? Why do many continue to believe these imbecilic claims when the failures of government are so obvious and their successes so obscure, questionable, and self-congratulatory?

Have not most religious *institutions* already promoted, as an unintended consequence, excessive personal irresponsibility for our human condition by anxiously waiting on pins and needles, for some 2,000 years, for a *future* event (second coming of Christ and Judgment) to rescue them from their plight? What hope do they have this event will happen in the next 2,000 years, the next two million years, or the next two billion years? How many more thousands of years will it take them to consider the *possibility* they've been vainly looking to the *future* for an event that may have already transpired? Isn't it quite ironic Christians find it easy to condemn those Jews who failed to acknowledge Christ's first coming when they themselves fail to acknowledge, or even consider the *possibility*, that His second coming may also be a past event? Isn't it conceivable that if Christ's first coming was missed by some His second coming may also have been missed by those whose hearts were blind to such an event?

Has not government recently co-opted the religious *institutions* to help quell potential civil unrest in the United States under the premise of "obeying the powers that be"? The *institution* of church and state is sadly alive and well in this current day and age, as it has been in past ages, even if the arrangement is less formal today. Both may be somewhat embarrassed, at times, with the symbiotic nature of their relationship, but nonetheless, they carry on with it while attempting to dress up the package in a wrapping of flags and crosses.

We determined to wipe the slate clean of previous thought and re-examine those premises we inherited, but did not accept ownership of, by <u>questioning authority</u> in every aspect of our lives to include the areas of religion, civil government, media, health care, food, finance, parenting, and education. The specific focus of this book is to question the interrelationships among religion, civil government, and our liberty — or lack thereof.

Some of our libertarian friends may be eager to ask at this point, "Aren't you just trading one form of bondage (bondage to the

State and religious *institutionalism*) for another form of bondage (bondage to God)?" That's a fair question. Most libertarians would agree that the key distinction between being either bond or free is whether *coercion* exists. The State, by its nature, exists by *coercive* means. God, on the other hand, simply exists. His power and omnipotence aren't contingent upon *coercion* or our acceptance of Him as Creator of the universe. So in answering the libertarian's question of whether we are trading one form of bondage for another, we would answer in the negative. In other words, absent *coercion* or fraud, there can be no bondage.

Religious *institutionalism* and the State subsist via the extracted life energies of others, whether that extraction of life energy is by force or fraud. Of the two forms of *coercion*, fraud is the far more dangerous to our liberty because where the mind goes, the body naturally follows. If we were forced to choose between giving up our physical liberty or our ability to think and reason, we would choose to give up our physical liberty and retain our ability to think and reason. Our true preference, of course, is the choice to liberate both mind and body from the tyranny of <u>all</u> *institutions*. And that is the purpose to which this book is devoted.

In every country and every age, the priest has been hostile to liberty. He is always in alliance with the despot, abetting his abuses in return for protection to his own. It is easier to acquire wealth and power by this combination than by deserving them, and to effect this, they have perverted the purest religion ever preached to man into mystery and jargon, unintelligible to all mankind, and therefore the safer for their purposes. – **Thomas Jefferson**

~

Chapter 1

Why Questioning is Important

Do not questions imply we have a choice? If we are traveling down a highway and come to a critical crossroad we think may significantly impact our journey in some way or another, we may choose to stop and ask for directions. When asking directions, or questioning the directions, doesn't this imply we have a choice to go this way or that way?

Isn't choice, in the above example, a manifestation of freedom and/or liberty? We can choose to go this way or that way. We are therefore free to choose, albeit within the limits set by the highway engineers. Maybe this explains the popularity of off-road vehicles. Intuitively, some people don't like artificial restraints on their comings and goings.

Fortunately, we have the ability to traverse multi-dimensionally through the landscape of our minds. We are not limited to going this way or that way because of structural limitations imposed on us by others. We do, however, often succumb to the efforts of others to control our mental journeys. There are many competing interests desiring to establish arbitrary highways and byways through the landscape of our minds in their desire to control our thought processes for their benefit. These interests use various forms of media to establish the mental roadways, traffic signals, on ramps, off ramps, and speed limits that condition us much like Pavlov's dogs to accept arbitrary options beneficial to them while only *superficially* beneficial to us. They desire to channel us down those mental pathways they've engineered, rather than allowing us the liberty of designing our own destiny.

In asking questions, are we not seeking truth? Conversely, if we are not asking questions, what is the default condition that often befalls us? For those who allow others to establish the highways and byways through the landscape of their minds, are they not placing themselves in a potential position of mental, spiritual, and physical servitude?

Why does the modern day slave master (nation state) seek to surreptitiously control the minds of those from whom they desire to extract life's energies? Is it because they realize slavery is much easier and more efficient if they first get control of their victim's mind? Is not the body more willing to go hither or thither when the mind is effectively harnessed with bit and bridle? The modern day slave master doesn't use a ball and chain, but he is no less effective than those pre-Civil War southern plantation owners were in the extraction of life energy from their respective subjects. And today, it's done without the negative stigma associated with a bygone era. Is not the most despicable slave the one who doesn't recognize he's a slave? If one doesn't recognize they are a slave, what hope do they have of escaping that horrid condition whereby their destiny is molded and shaped by the mind of someone else?

Is not <u>questioning</u> the crucial mechanism we use to develop <u>our own</u> belief system? Is not questioning how we seek and discover truth? And isn't personal liberty a by-product of seeking and applying truth to our own lives?

If we don't seek to discover truth, would it not be a fair statement to say that we obviously don't value truth enough to expend the energy in its acquisition? For that matter, isn't how we choose to expend our precious life energy the ultimate barometer of what we value the most?

How many of us have been guilty of lazily turning over our minds to those who desire our energies to be expended for their benefit? How many of us question the media spin we are bombarded with on television each day? How many of us question how our children's minds are molded and shaped by the mental engineers in public schools? How does it make you feel knowing, or not knowing, the values of those people who spend 6 hours or more each day creating the highways and byways through your child's mind?

Is not the act of questioning the key to our personal and spiritual survival, as it represents the discovery mechanism for truth? Conversely, would it not be the goal of tyrants to convince us to dispense with questioning their *authority* and to dispense with seeking truth outside their sphere of control?

Does not the Internet represent a social sphere or realm the Statists have yet to figure out how to control? Will they be able to put the Internet Genie back in the bottle? Does not the Internet, much like the printing press did, give individuals the opportunity for personal and spiritual sovereignty without having to go through an earthbound high priest who puts his pants on one leg at a time just like the rest of us do?

A modern day example that portrays the power of the Internet to undermine centralized control of information and political power, in much the same fashion the printing press facilitated the Reformation and undermined centralized authority of the Catholic Church, was the very successful Internet campaign and fundraising effort by supporters of Ron Paul during the 2008 presidential campaign. The Internet campaign and fundraising effort were truly spontaneous, grass roots, and unprecedented in the number of dollars accumulated in a single 24-hour period. Ron Paul's political opponents tried to replicate it for their own campaigns, but they were unsuccessful because they attempted to use a top-down centralized model and failed in their attempt to harness the energy, vibrancy, and loyal Internet following that was spontaneously generated around the globe by his supporters.

The powerful elite were clearly envious of Ron Paul's Internet fame, and Ron's un-engineered success in this arena was a shot across the bow of the Republican Party and the mainstream media's centralized top-down approach to control and dissemination of information. The Republican Party, along with so-called conservative media pundits, in the aftermath of the 2008 elections, are now scratching and clawing to regain their lost credibility. Mainstream media is now hosting Ron Paul at every opportunity, and they even allow him to finish his sentences without rudely interrupting him. Everything Ron Paul said about the economy during the campaign is coming to fruition. The mainstream media pundits who mocked Ron during the campaign seem now to be awakening from their stupor. Are they deathly afraid their miscalculation of the power of the Internet will make their rendition of television news obsolete in much the same fashion newspaper publishing companies are becoming obsolete and disappearing faster than fish wrap on a hot humid summer afternoon?

The Internet will probably be increasingly vilified by governments and religious *authoritarians*, as being a tool for terror and sin when, in fact, it is being used as a tool for freedom, much to the dismay of Statists and religious *authoritarians* around the world. These high priests of the secular and religious world are being effectively defrocked in the minds of those actively engaged in the *journey* of seeking truth through effective questioning.

Is not the quality of our belief system (truthful answers to life's critical questions) hinged on the quality of the questions we ask of ourselves continually? Is it really reasonable to expect that our belief system can exceed in superiority the quality of the questions we pose to it?

If we have beliefs, or a belief system, not based upon questions we have asked of ourselves, are we not holding to beliefs based upon the questions or assertions of others? If we believe we are all truly equal, by what measure of confidence can we assume their questions and/or assertions will be superior to our own?

If our belief system is primarily based upon the questions and assertions of others instead of our own, do we truly own those beliefs or do we become mindless drones parroting the mantra scripted for us by the mind of someone else?

If we do not own our beliefs, are we not ascribing our value, our self-worth, and our life's potential to others and in doing so shackling our minds in a state of voluntary mental servitude while forsaking our personal responsibility to use the gifts (our mind and reasoning ability) our Creator has endowed us with?

Is it not doubly deplorable when we unquestioningly accept the beliefs of others but also attempt to defend those beliefs we have not validated through the questioning process? Would that not be akin to the plantation slave justifying, in defense of the slave owner, why he is a slave?

Which individual should garner our admiration the most, an individual owning, through questioning, what we perceive as a flawed viewpoint or an individual who inherits and adopts what we perceive as a more truthful viewpoint but does so without questioning? Is not the latter's viewpoint an accident of birth, while the former's viewpoint is one of an individual acting with purpose and intent?

Is there a more deplorable condition of humanity than a man or woman without a purpose? How many of us wait until we are on our deathbed before asking the vital question of life's purpose? How many die with this question on their lips, while leaving it unanswered?

A man or woman *with purpose* questions and examines everything. A man or woman *with purpose* is quick to reject those beliefs not able to endure the questioning process.

Is not a primary purpose of our existence on this earth to seek and discover truth and integrate it into our very essence and being with the utmost sobriety? If we perceive the discovery of truth as being a *journey* rather than a *destination*, would the questioning process ever end or would we continue questioning until we draw our last breath?

We believe the questioning process and questioning man-conceived authority are the only relevant vehicles available to us in seeking truth and its by-products, freedom and liberty. The challenge we are all faced with is how to ask better and more empowering questions. Much too often, the power elite will effectively frame the discussion to purposefully exclude those options threatening their capacity for growth and power. The *Statist* model can only grow and expand at the expense of personal liberty.

He who asks a question is a fool for five minutes; he who does not ask a question is a fool forever. - **Chinese Proverb**

~

Chapter 2

What is Truth?

Philosophers down through the ages have waxed eloquent on this question with varying degrees of success. We will attempt to avoid getting caught up in that quagmire during this discussion and examine the subject by approaching it a little differently.

We simply wish to define what truth is for the purpose of continuing our discussion on a level playing field of understanding. Whether or not the reader ultimately agrees with our definition of "truth" isn't as relevant as the understanding of our use of the word throughout the rest of the book.

We, therefore, wish to define truth simply as...*the absence of lies.* We believe this definition of truth is one in which most of us can agree, regardless of our upbringing, education, political persuasion, or religious indoctrination and it serves as a building block for continuing our dialogue.

Can lies and truth occupy the same space, or does one have to be discarded before the other can be acquired? Lies and truth are much like oil and water...they don't mix.

Therefore, should not our journey through life ideally represent the continual rejection of lies for the acquisition of truth? Ideally, this process of rejecting lies and acquiring truth doesn't end until we take our last breath. Does not the spirit need food all the way to the end, just as the body does? Is not truth what nourishes the spirit? If the continual seeking and acquisition of truth <u>does</u> end before our body dies, will not the spirit shrivel up and die?

Is truth relative?

We must distinguish the difference between the use of the word truth and its plural…truths.

The *truth*, in the singular, implies an all-encompassing position, while the word *truths* suggest a plurality within the greater context of the truth. For example, if an observer happened to be standing eyeball to kneecap with an elephant, it would be *a* truth to point to the elephant's kneecap and call it a kneecap. If another observer happened to be standing a further distance off, it would be a more encompassing truth to point at the elephant itself and call it an elephant. Both observations, although true, might appear to be at variance with each other. Of course, this isn't a perfect example of what we are trying to convey, because an observer standing even further back might not just see one elephant, but a whole herd of elephants. As inadequate as our illustration may be, we believe we've made the point that there are those truths, in part, which belong to a greater and more encompassing truth. If both observers happened to be viewing the elephant from nearly the same exact location and at the same time, one would expect there to be little variance in the descriptive terms used, and both observers could begin discussing the specifics of their individual observations from a mutual point of view.

So, truth can be *relative* to the observer of it, depending upon their relative vantage point.

For another example, an individual living in Ecuador (at the equator) enjoys an equal number of hours of daylight and darkness each of the 365 days a year and can truthfully proclaim there are 12 hours of light and 12 hours of darkness each and every day of the year. An Eskimo, on the other hand, living in Barrow, Alaska, has 85 continuous days each year in which there is no darkness. The Eskimo can truthfully proclaim, from his or her vantage point, that the hours of daylight and darkness vary significantly throughout the year. Both the Eskimo and the Ecuadorian are telling *a* truth from their respective vantage points, but they are saying something also that is quite different and possibly foreign to each other's knowledge base. Both of them could no doubt have heated discussions if they were to discuss their observations in *absolute* terms.

The obvious danger, of course, is when individuals and/or societies discover what they believe to be an <u>encompassing</u> truth when, in reality, it is only a truth <u>in part</u>, or worse yet, no truth at all. On a strictly individual basis, the only person to suffer a misapplied *partial* truth, or a lie, is the person who believes it. Sadly, however, many people who believe they have the truth are seldom satisfied with maintaining a sole proprietorship of the truth and want, instead, to convert the heathens, savages, and those with lesser intellect to their cherished and superior flat earth dogmas. They believe they must defend the truth and are quite willing to employ political coercion to do so when the more appropriate and Biblically sanctioned action would be the practice of the golden rule (a rapidly fading Christian principle) in which we *live and let live*. Treating others as we would like to be treated is at the core of libertarian thought and the teachings of Jesus Christ. Quite interestingly, those in the libertarian camp have historically practiced the golden rule much more stringently than those in the religious *institutions* have, even though the gap appears to be narrowing recently with more and more libertarians jumping on the war bandwagon with many of their neighbors who call themselves Christians.

Much too often, the vast chasm between talking the truth and living it points to the rather obvious fact that we <u>all</u> are simply human. To pretend otherwise is to deceive ourselves. Recognizing our own human frailties is what should keep us all humble and even less susceptible to the frailties of our neighbors. To allow other humans to assume positions of power and authority over our spiritual or physical condition, knowing that they, too, put their pants on one leg at a time, is pure folly and totally irresponsible. Likewise, for another human to <u>assume</u> a position of power and authority over the spiritual or physical condition of their neighbor is unmitigated arrogance. After all, how often have Christians endured the accusation of being called hypocrites because they failed to live up to or walk the church talk? Think about it for a moment. If one could only convert the heathen by how they themselves lived their religion Monday through Saturday, how would things tally out? In following the churchgoer's Monday through Saturday example, how many people would get it? The truthful answer to that question may explain why some feel so compelled to preach it or pay others to do so.

Does the truth need defending?

Many of us may have grown up with the idea that we have to stand up for and defend the truth. Is the truth that weak that it needs <u>man</u> to defend it? How can we defend what we are still discovering? Mankind has enough trouble simply seeking truth and living within its boundaries without being saddled with the additional mission of defending it.

We can probably all agree that the law of gravity is a universal truth, but do we need to defend it?

We believe a particular truth is perfectly capable of defending itself for those naïve enough to dare challenge it. Try jumping out of an airplane without a parachute and see if truth (law of gravity) prevails or not. No, the law of gravity does not need defending. Truth is perfectly capable of its own defense!

The danger we face in attempting to defend what we perceive to be the truth is that our focus is <u>less</u> on *d-i-s-c-o-v-e-r-y* of truth and <u>more</u> on *maintaining* our current beliefs. Don't we, in attempting to defend what we perceive to be a truth, tend to grasp it tighter and tighter, as if we are fearful it might somehow escape our control? If we cling tightfistedly to our old models, how likely are we to release them for a better model? If we are clinging tightfistedly to our old models, will we even be looking for a new model? What chance do we have for personal growth if we believe truth is a destination we've arrived at long ago? Would not a more empowering and liberating belief encourage us to seek truth continually?

If what we are grasping as a truth, with a white knuckle grip, <u>is</u> the truth, releasing our tight grip on it won't endanger it or increase the odds that we will lose it. Truth has eternal and omnipotent characteristics and will still be there tomorrow, just like the law of gravity.

A lie, unlike a truth, always needs defending, lest the purveyors of that lie run out of fresh suckers to fleece. A lie, once recognized as such, doesn't enjoy much repeat business unless force is involved or the buyer of the lie is convinced, via fraud, that there is some greater good to come to society by the continuance of it. The purveyors and defenders of lies are <u>men</u>.

A truth, on the other hand, always has willing and returning customers. A truth doesn't need force or fraud, or new suckers for its sustenance. Truth is a standalone. It doesn't need us to defend it. It doesn't want our feeble defense. Man doesn't have enough credibility to defend the truth. How can we defend what we are still discovering? Yesterday's *truth* (the earth is flat) is tomorrow's joke.

Don't most misunderstandings between people arise when discussions are jump started without the benefit of the other person's viewpoint or, at a minimum, agreeing on the definition of terms being used? The old admonishment, "Don't judge a man until you've walked a mile in his moccasins" often applies, but is less frequently adhered to.

We believe most readers will agree with us when we say lies hold no value for those who unwittingly find themselves possessing them. Lies, much like lemon automobiles, are to be sold rather than bought. Lies do have value to those purveyors subsisting on them at the expense of the naive.

We've all bought lies from time to time because no one has arrived at that state or condition of having all truth. A person cannot have all truth within a lifetime. Otherwise, we would not have fallen victim to the used car dealer who knowingly sold us a lemon or the hedge fund manager who conned us into buying a mirror image of an asset (derivative). If we had all truth, we would not have fallen victim to the promises of various political candidates who sold us the big lie that the government would put a chicken in every pot without raising taxes. If we had all truth, we would not have fallen victim to the bank run of 1929; the savings and loan debacle of the 1980s; the current banking crisis; and the Social Security Ponzi scheme.

In order to buy a lie, one has to sell a corresponding truth. One of the biggest lies is the one implying that *we can have something for nothing*. The corresponding truth trumping this lie is that *there is no free lunch*. The unwinding of the current financial crisis we find ourselves in suggests we may today be paying for yesterday's proverbial free lunch. Some may say, "Wait a minute, I'm not a hedge fund manager or banker so don't blame me. I didn't do anything wrong." No, maybe not. But many placed far too much confidence in others (human *authority*) to protect them from such a calamity and are paying a dear price for their misplaced faith. What many fail to realize is the price paid was just a down payment, and the swindle continues to be a crime in progress.

Many place far too much confidence in government (human *authority*) to protect them from fraudulent financial practices without realizing that government itself is one of the biggest purveyors and facilitators of financial fraud. We need look no further than the Social Security Ponzi scheme or our Federal Reserve banking system to see that private banking interests, in partnership with a wayward government, created the framework and corrupt model for corporations to pattern themselves after. If a Ponzi scheme is immoral and fraudulent for individuals and corporations to pawn on a gullible public, by what miraculous transformation does a Social Security Ponzi scheme or a fractional reserve banking system somehow gain a deified sense of morality just because the government blesses it?

When a crime is defined not so much by its elements, but rather is overshadowed by its many exceptions effectively exempting some classes and categories of individuals from a given criminal act while punishing others for the same act, does not the law and those administering it become braying and somewhat annoying jackasses to the rest of us who simply wish to be left alone?

Buy the truth, and sell it not; also wisdom, and instruction, and understanding. - **Proverbs 23:23**

~

Chapter 3

Relationship of Truth to Belief

We've defined truth as the absence of lies. We would now like to distinguish truth from belief. Belief is commonly defined as…***something that is accepted as true.***

Everyone has beliefs and beliefs are necessary to continue life. Without beliefs, would we even get up out of bed in the morning?

Although we generally accept our beliefs as true, it doesn't mean they are, in fact, true. For example, at one point in history the wise ones of the world *believed* the earth was flat. Many held to this erroneous viewpoint for quite some time. As long as they didn't coercively apply this erroneous and flawed viewpoint onto others, it was a belief that only restricted the liberty of those who held it.

No one really wants to admit the beliefs they hold are not true. The barrier to dropping a flawed belief for a better one often depends upon how many other "contingent" beliefs we've stacked on top of the former. Thus, the barrier to implementing change in one's life is often contingent on what the change will *cost* rather than the *merits* of its relationship to truth. What we sometimes neglect to consider, as we weigh the cost of trading a flawed belief for a better one, is the cost of clinging to a belief devoid of truth. Our beliefs represent the framework of "accepted truths" that influence and guide our decision making process as we go about the dynamics of living. The truthfulness of those beliefs determines the quality of our lives, as our beliefs continually drive the choices we make. The cumulative choices we make ultimately determine our own personal destinies. If our beliefs are devoid of truth, our choices become much more restricted, and our destinies fall short of our intent. Truthful beliefs, on the other hand, expand our options on the future and lead us to our goals. When we consider the significant impact our beliefs have on the quality of our lives and our interactions with our fellow man, there should be no price too great in the seeking and acquisition of truth.

When we consider how many people have a part to play in the forming of our personal belief systems, including parents, teachers, preachers, lawyers, stock brokers, doctors, dentists, judges, bankers, presidents, congressmen, movie celebrities, and news media personalities, it becomes readily apparent our belief system can easily be made up of a hodgepodge of ideas that can take a lifetime to sort through, categorize, accept, reject, or implement with any degree of confidence. How many of us fully realize the importance of questioning *authority* and long-held beliefs until such time we are suddenly faced with a calamity spawned from a flawed belief system and associated choices? Just exploring the diversity of strongly held beliefs among those attending a small family gathering or family reunion can lend itself to some interesting projections related to diversity of beliefs encountered on a much larger scale.

For those who never question *authority*, life is simple. The *authorities* closest to them massage their belief systems and, consequently, influence their choices and personal destinies. Those ruled over in such a manner mimic the mindless beasts of the field that are channeled here or there at the behest of someone else's mind. This is not an unusual phenomenon, as history is replete with erroneous beliefs that were strongly held and propagated for several generations before some inquisitive soul, by questioning *authority*, dispelled them. At one time, the *authorities* believed the earth was flat, heavier objects fell faster than lighter objects, and, more recently, that a nation can spend and consume itself into prosperity.

We readily admit we can't do everything ourselves and that we may need to delegate some of life's tasks out to others, but how much should we delegate? To whom should we delegate? Who is ultimately responsible for our delegation decisions? Who will ultimately pay the price for mistaken beliefs? Who, ultimately, has the greatest proprietary interest in our personal well-being? Are we easily impressed by credentials and licensure issued by governmental bodies, or by actual performance?

The more intermediaries we have between ourselves and what is vitally important to us for life's sustenance and happiness, the greater the risk of default. This is an area of our lives that requires constant re-evaluation because of the cyclical nature of society's values. Honor, trust, and confidence among individuals and *institutions* can easily be thrown under the bus when society's core values are in a state of decline.

What is the relationship between <u>fear</u> and our beliefs?

The beliefs we've never tested and completely validated on our own, by answering each and every challenge, are the ones that cause us the most fear. If we don't fully own our beliefs we fear those who challenge them and will be more likely to put up an obstinate defense. When we truly own our beliefs through examination and due diligence, we are less fearful of challenges, because we know those challenging our beliefs will not likely be able to ask any questions we have not already considered. This attitude toward having our beliefs challenged has multiple benefits. First of all, we can afford to be polite and courteous and demonstrate to those challenging us that we are more interested in pursuing truth than defending our beliefs. Secondly, it gives us the opportunity of considering another point of view. It may be entirely within the realm of possibility that we've missed a vital question during the conduct of our own personal due diligence, and we may find a re-examination of our belief to be in order. We believe the end game is not to <u>defend</u> our beliefs, but rather to <u>examine</u> them continually. When we examine our beliefs continually, are we not showing, by example, the importance of continually seeking truth?

If we inherit an inferior belief and never validate its relevance to our own lives, we've automatically accepted the limitations it imposes on our capacity for freedom.

How often do men and women tyrannize themselves with their false beliefs and freedom-limiting choices while, at the same time, decrying the tyranny imposed on them by government? If men and women were more honest with themselves on this point, would it not place them, for the most part, in a much better position to mitigate governmental tyranny? What tyranny, whether self-imposed or government-imposed, can't be mitigated by exercising our minds, withdrawing our consent, and making choices consistent with a better and more truthful belief, even if that means voting with our feet and moving elsewhere? Is not freedom, therefore, acquired by continually seeking truth, altering our flawed belief systems, and making choices that expand future options?

> *Poor, wretched, and stupid peoples, nations determined on your own misfortune and blind to your own good! You let yourselves be deprived before your own eyes of the best part of your revenues; your fields are plundered, your homes robbed, your family heirlooms taken away. You live in such a way that you cannot claim a single thing as your own; and it would seem that you consider yourselves lucky to be loaned your property, your families,*

and your very lives. All this havoc, this misfortune, this ruin, descends upon you not from alien foes, but from the one enemy whom you yourselves render as powerful as he is, for whom you go bravely for war, for whose greatness you do not refuse to offer your own bodies unto death. He who thus domineers over you has only two eyes, only two hands, only one body, no more than is possessed by the least man among the infinite numbers dwelling in your cities; he has indeed nothing more than the power that you confer upon him to destroy you. Where has he acquired enough eyes to spy upon you, if you do not provide them yourselves? How can he have so many arms to beat you with, if he does not borrow them from you? The feet that trample down your cities, where does he get them if they are not your own? How does he have any power over you except through you? How would he dare assail you if he had no cooperation from you? What could he do to you if you yourselves did not connive with the thief who plunders you, if you were not accomplices of the murderer who kills you, if you were not traitors to yourselves? You sow your crops in order that he may ravage them, you install and furnish your homes to give him goods to pillage; you rear your daughters that he may gratify his lust; you bring up your children in order that he may confer upon them the greatest privilege he knows – to be led into his battles, to be delivered to butchery, to be made the servants of his greed and the instruments of his vengeance; you yield your bodies unto hard labor in order that he may indulge in his delights and wallow in his filthy pleasures; you weaken yourselves in order to make him the stronger and the mightier to hold you in check. From all these indignities, such as the very beasts of the field would not endure, you can deliver yourselves if you try, not by taking action, but merely by willing to be free. Resolve to serve no more, and you are at once freed. I do not ask that you place hands upon the tyrant to topple him over, but simply that you support him no longer; then you will behold him, like a great Colossus whose pedestal has been pulled away, fall of his own weight and break into pieces. – **Etienne De La Boetie,** ***The Politics of Obedience; The Discourse of Voluntary Servitude* circa 1552**

The prison bricks composing our personal prisons and limiting our capacity for freedom are made of lies. These prisons we find ourselves in, or build ourselves, are constructed one lie at a time. With each brick's placement, there is a corresponding truth that has been cast away as rubble. Each truth we embrace, on the other hand, turns a prison brick made of a lie to dust and blows away with the wind. If truth is not appropriately valued and we embrace lies, our loss of freedom becomes the default condition, and prison becomes our status quo.

Many of us are born into these prisons when we inherit the false beliefs of others. We often approach adulthood and independence from the family unit with a significant portion of our personal prisons built up around us with the false beliefs and lies transferred to us from government schools, religious *institutions*, our parents, and personal associations. In some cases, the lies composing our prisons are transferred to us with purpose and intent by those with evil intent. In other instances, these lies are transferred to us by those who were themselves born into a prison composed of the false beliefs of other men.

A vital mission in life, if we choose to accept it, has two parts. First, we must accept the *possibility* we may be erroneously holding to false beliefs, to our own detriment and imprisonment. Second, we must re-validate long-held beliefs by questioning and discarding all of them that don't bear up under scrutiny.

When we blindly adopt a religion, a political system, a literary dogma, we become automatons. We cease to grow. – **Anais Nin**

Chapter 4

The END TIMES Hoax

Don't most people unequivocally accept the idea that the second coming of Christ is a *future* event? Upon what basis is this idea almost universally accepted? Is there a scriptural basis for this assumption? Is it ever questioned? Have you validated this widely held assumption? What impact does this assumption have on your life? How has it affected your liberty? Has it influenced your willingness to accept coercive *institutions* as a continuation of the divine right of kings doctrine? Has the promotion of this doctrine, by religious *institutions,* contributed to a shift in loyalties away from God and more toward men? Who benefits the most from its perpetuation? The authors of this book neglected to ask these very questions of themselves for over 50 years.

We've laughingly discussed the period in history before, during, and after The Dark Ages and have shaken our heads in absolute disbelief that for 2,000 years, mankind held fast to the erroneous belief that heavier objects, when dropped, fell faster than lighter objects. People unequivocally accepted Aristotle's law of falling bodies as fact. No one, for roughly 2,000 years, had enough curiosity to challenge or question this fallacy by conducting a simple experiment. They simply accepted Aristotle as the *authority* on the subject. Each succeeding generation inherited this fallacious concept and continued its perpetuation by *indoctrinating* the following generation. And on and on it went.

Well, we are no longer snickering at Aristotle or the dim bulbs that followed him. We, too, have played the part of dim bulbs in the spiritual realm, by unquestioningly accepting, for over 50 years, the belief that the second coming of Christ is a *future* event.

We couldn't point to scripture to support our inherited viewpoint, but instead, deferred to *authorities* who've supposedly studied the issue in depth. Many of these *authorities* have approached their study predisposed to the idea that the second coming of Christ is a *future* event and their study was therefore limited to the parameters and scope of their biases, creed, and/or to scripture taken out of context. Their efforts appear to be more driven by a need to defend those biases and creeds than being a genuine and sincere search for the truth. Most often, the *authorities* have already discovered the truth and, therefore, have limited opportunity for future discovery and associated benefits. Being an *authority* on any subject can effectively place its victim in a box from which there is little to no opportunity for escape. Such *authorities* can easily find themselves serving life sentences married to an idea that may only stand the test within the confines of their own minds. Being an *authority* on any subject is not an enviable position, but it is even less so in the spiritual realm because of the grave consequences for being wrong, in and of itself, and the additional consequences for potentially misleading others. What if, for example, one dies and crosses over to the other side only to discover the creed they lived by was the wrong model, and many people followed after them in error? Will they receive recompense for being wrong and an additional portion of punishment for misleading others? It's a sobering thought for wannabe *authorities* or to those who allow themselves to be thrust into such a position by those disinclined to search and sift these things out on their own.

Some may argue they don't cling to creeds and that they <u>only</u> follow the Bible. Well, they are in very generous company these days, because the vast majority of denominations and so-called non-denominations make a similar claim but have, at the same time, significant doctrinal differences that effectively make one or the other of them hell-bound. The *futurist* creed, however, is the <u>one</u> creed they almost all unwaveringly accept while they endlessly debate and war with one another over their uniquely intricate and opposing doctrines without realizing they were spawned from the same *futurist* source. These doctrinal debates would succumb to a natural and fitting death if they just gave the *futurist* creed the same devoted and intense examination they've given to these less important spin-off issues.

We hope it is needless to say this, but in case you've not already guessed it, we don't want to be labeled *authorities* on this subject or any other subject. We would like to leave room for the discovery of truth and personal growth in this journey we call life. Some readers may have already dismissed what we have to say simply because the basic premise of our work is so far outside the bounds of traditional *institutional* thought patterns. We'll take that as a compliment and continue on in sharing our thoughts with those of you who are still with us and to those brave souls who may be inclined, later, to conduct a simple experiment that we believe will prove to be immensely rewarding in this life and the next.

This work is dedicated to those curious souls who are not fearful of questioning *authority* and long-held beliefs, especially those long-held beliefs that were inherited. Just because we may have been born in the back seat of a Ford does not mean we have to drive one the rest of our lives. If we choose to drive a Ford, it should probably be based on better rationale. Quite ironically, we usually give far more thought to the intricacies and complexities of choosing, purchasing, and financing an automobile than we give to the beliefs we've inherited. These inherited beliefs are passively accepted, but if they are the foundation upon which other beliefs are stacked, we have a responsibility to determine if those beliefs will support them.

It is our contention that the second coming of Christ, as a *future* event, is a man-conceived creed, without scriptural basis, and that this almost universal creed is currently a product of momentum rather than any serious consideration of scripture. At its inception, however, there is a high degree of likelihood that the seemingly unending supply of wannabe *Statists* and religious *authoritarians* who desired to regain political and religious control after A.D. 70 wasted no time in making their mutually supportive aspirations a reality through the use of the tools of force and fraud that Christ had previously liberated His followers from at His second coming during the judgment and destruction of Jerusalem in A.D. 70. This would also explain why the book of Revelation is generally segregated from the rest of the New Testament in the minds of those who accept the *futurist* creed without question. This segregation of the book of Revelation from the rest of the New Testament is also manifested in the way the book of Revelation is traditionally portrayed as not being understandable. Many people won't even read Revelation because of the ooh-wah ooh-wah nature of the language used. The book of Revelation is often discarded into the *too hard to do bin* along with much of the Old Testament.

Christians pride themselves in primarily studying the New Testament because the Old Testament and old law were for God's chosen people in a different time and place. But how many of these same Christians will quickly defend the concept of preemptively killing, without provocation, their neighbors in faraway lands based on Old Testament examples? Did they forget that God directly intervened in those battles for a very express purpose that was ultimately fulfilled with the death, burial, and resurrection of Christ and with the restoration of God's sovereign authority in A.D. 70?

How many claiming to be New Testament Christians are able to produce any New Testament examples to support their ideology that murderous rampages around the globe, in which hundreds of thousands of innocent men, women, and children are purposefully starved to death or slaughtered is consistent with the teaching and example of Jesus Christ and the New Testament (John 18:36; II Corinthians 10:3-4)? And how many of them continue to participate in political elections where they will vote for those who seem obsessed and crazed with that blood-soaked ideology?

The authors formerly held this very ideology, but they held to it ever more grudgingly over the years until they finally discarded it altogether after finally finding the answers to those nagging questions that haunted them continually. We were not satisfied with the commonly given fall back explanation that there are some things we won't know the answers to until we get to heaven. Keeping to that track might have an entirely different destination. We kept seeking the answers to the questions that haunted us, and this work is a culmination of that effort.

A neglectful approach toward the study of the Old Testament contributes greatly to the lack of understanding of the book of Revelation. The Jews and Gentiles who believed in Christ understood perfectly what the book of Revelation meant.

This neglect, combined with the overall study of the Bible with the predisposition that the second coming of Christ is a *future* event only compounds the misunderstanding. This misunderstanding leads to comments like, "It is not really that important if Christ came in A.D. 70, or if it's some *future* date. The most important thing is that we are ready for our own personal judgment." We agree that being <u>ready</u> is vitally important, but what is being <u>ready</u> all about? We contend one may have difficulty being truly <u>ready</u> until they face this study of Christ's second coming head-on with serious personal study, instead of that dispensed by the *authorities*. If one reads what the *authorities* have to say about it, and if they read it really fast and without a whole lot of thought, it doesn't sound too bad. But if you slow it down a bit and think on it, it can also sound strangely alien and incongruent with the Bible they claim as being the inspired word of God. Ultimately, the predisposition of thought (the belief) that the second coming of Christ is a *future* event serves as a belief filter that predisposes and limits the outcome of the study. The Bible reads so much differently with this limiting filter installed, and there is no scriptural basis for its existence. Absent a scriptural basis for this filter, does it not become simply another man-conceived creed among so many others of no lesser or greater value?

The authors, too, have their biases, and we don't pretend for a moment to think that we've removed all our limiting filters. Generally speaking, only the *authorities* and some of their followers pretend to have removed all prejudicial thinking from their study of the Bible. We make no such claim. As part of this study, we are going to ask you to remove your filter that the second coming of Christ is a *future event* and ask you to install a new filter that predisposes you to the concept that the second coming of Christ is a *past event,* and it took place at the destruction of Jerusalem in A.D. 70. We ask that you bear with us and pretend it has already happened. As an illustration, if we were to take the reader on an elephant hunt, it would be vitally important the reader, at a minimum, believed in the *possibility* of the existence of this creature. Otherwise, one could be standing right next to it and not recognize it for what it truly is. In this instance, most have been conditioned to believe no such creature or possibility exists.

Most people, by default, have excluded the possibility the second coming of Christ is a past event and have repeatedly read the Bible over and over again with this clogged and prejudicial filter in place. Reading the Bible through just once with the new filter in place will overwhelmingly convince the reader to forever discard the old filter. Conducting this experiment will be the equivalent of personally stepping outside and dropping a large rock and a small rock to validate, or not, a long-held belief and doing so without relying on an *authority* figure to monitor and influence progress and outcome.

Since the *futurist* point of view has been so ingrained and inculcated into our core belief system without question, it is necessary to approach this exercise with an excitedly different filter in place to fully appreciate the contrast. This new filter has the capacity to challenge our thinking and approach to studying the Bible. This new filter has the capacity to ignite and renew in us a hungering and thirsting for truth wherever it leads. This new filter has the power to change the world. This new filter offers much more liberty, hope, and promise in this life and the hereafter. This new filter of liberty is the antithesis to the old filter of bondage from which Christ came to liberate us. This new filter effectively transfers the power and authority we've carelessly delegated to others, in every aspect of our lives, back to where it rightfully belongs.

The *futurist* creed has generated much confusion and disputation among many generally likeminded Christians over the subject of millennialism, the *last days* prophecy, support of the state of Israel and promotion of war and genocide against non-Christians as well as those who don't support American interests.

The book of Revelation was written in *future* tense because it described a *future* event to the original audience. In order to understand any passage of scripture, it is necessary to know <u>who</u> it was written to and for what purpose. The book of Revelation describes the events associated with the judgment of those profane shepherds (religious leaders) who rejected God's authority and also those profane religious leaders (chief priests, Pharisees, and Sadducees) who were responsible for oppressing and killing the prophets, persecuting and killing the apostles and disciples, and crucifying Christ (John 19:15). The book of Revelation also describes the destruction and fall of Jerusalem along with the advent of a new heaven and a new earth and the restoration of God as being the only authorized sovereign among His people. No longer would God use kings and kingdoms of men, because the *reformation, restitution,* and *refreshing* (Acts 3:19-21; Hebrews 9:8-10) was accomplished with the complete ushering in of the kingdom of God and the new covenant when the Judaic Age was closed out with the destruction of the tabernacle and Jerusalem in A.D. 70. In order to understand the book of Revelation, it must be read as a book of history. The book of Revelation is the <u>history</u> of the *end times* of the Judaic world as they knew it.

The *futurist* creed promotes institutional *authority* worship in both the religious and secular realm, with the predictable result of diminished personal responsibility across a wide spectrum of one's life. Personal responsibility gives way to a Nanny State style caretaking role in which those being cared for come to rely on all *authorities* to such an extreme extent that they set aside their innate physical and spiritual self-preservation mechanisms. Is not the unwarranted reverence for human *authority* figures the chief cause of human exploitation and suffering around the world and throughout the history of mankind?

It may be easier for many to see institutional *authority* worship in the Catholic Church because of the scripturally illegitimate reverence shown the Pope by Catholics. Less evident, but equally without scriptural basis, is the reverence many have for preachers, pastors, elders and deacons. In either case, however, if one questions institutional *authority,* they're considered to have blasphemed the Holy Spirit. The only time this Holy Grail attitude is questioned is when a Catholic priest is found guilty of sexually abusing a small child or when a preacher, pastor, elder, or deacon runs off with the church secretary or gets arrested for some un-Christian activity that brings shame and reproach upon that *institution*. Only then does it become glaringly apparent that Catholic priests and protestant preachers, pastors, elders, and deacons are human, just like the rest of us.

The stark reality, obscured by *institutional* group think, is that God never intended man to be ruled by man. Let's repeat that one more time. God never intended man to be ruled by man. *Gifted* men <u>did</u> oversee the Lord's work during the Christian dispensation, but they had spiritual *gifts* that men don't have today. Furthermore, during the Christian dispensation, these men or elders were appointed by *gifted* and *inspired* apostles and disciples. How many elders today can claim to be *gifted* or appointed by *inspired* apostles or disciples? A few evangelicals might make the claim in some of their tent revival meetings, but they are easily brought back to reality when a <u>real</u> invalid approaches them to be healed of a withered arm or leg. And others might claim to have this *authority*, but only in the spiritual realm and without the power to physically heal. You ask them, "And what makes you so special?" And they reply, "I was appointed or ordained an elder." We ask, "By whom and by what authority?" In reality, the best answer they can give is, "By uninspired human authority." If they followed the New Testament example, they would be appointed by *gifted* and *inspired* apostles or disciples and would have special powers to heal and cast out devils. In following New Testament example, it's all or nothing. It's either the real deal, as portrayed in New

Testament example, or fiction. If there is no New Testament example of *uninspired* and *ungifted men* handling the spiritual affairs of those in their congregations, by what authority do *uninspired* and *ungifted* men assume such a position in modern day congregations?

A common rationalization to offset or explain away the issue of why miraculous powers and gifts are no longer manifested in this day and age is that God doesn't need to work in miraculous ways today because we have the Bible, which is the inspired word of God. The unspoken and unintended implication with this position is that the authors of these original letters were not inspired. We beg to differ. We contend that the words of the prophets and these letters were truly inspired, and no one holding fast to the principle the Bible is the inspired word of God can seriously disagree with that premise without shooting themselves in both feet with very large cannons.

- II Timothy 3:16 – All scripture is given by inspiration of God
- Acts 1:16 – Scripture (prophecy) fulfilled came from the Holy Ghost via David
- Acts 3:18 – Things God showed via the mouth of His prophets
- Luke 21:14-15 – Christ to put words in the mouth of His disciples
- Mark 13:11 – Holy Ghost to speak through the disciples
- Luke 12:11-12 – Holy Ghost to teach disciples what to say
- I Peter 1:12 – Holy Ghost as a critical component of preaching

[Special Note: Throughout this book all references to Biblical scripture and associated commentary are based on the King James Version.]

These <u>inspired</u> letters the authors wrote were delivered to the congregations they were addressing. Often times, these letters referenced the <u>inspired</u> scriptures of prophecy (Old Testament). If those letters were not inspired, how could the Bible be inspired? Did something magically happen at the publishing house a thousand or more years later after the printing press was invented? If so, what happened to all those people after the destruction of Jerusalem and for the next fourteen hundred years or so who didn't have a copy of the Bible (66 bound books) or the benefit of witnessing firsthand the miraculous works and preaching of the apostles and disciples who had long been deceased? Did God abandon those people, or did he just leave it in the Pope's hands? We contend God neither abandoned those people nor left the Pope in charge of it.

The Bible, which contains <u>some</u> of the writings of the prophets and the apostles, didn't all of a sudden become blessed as the inspired word of God when it was bound up in its leather binding at the publishing company a thousand or more years later. The Bible is simply a collection of what once <u>was</u> *inspired* writings and bound together after *uninspired* human translators, with any number of biases, began tinkering with it. How many of us can really justify studying the Bible without having a Hebrew and Greek dictionary available to help us sort through the biases and prejudices of these *uninspired* translators?

Many people would agree that miraculous interventions ended with the death of the *gifted* apostles and with those to whom these gifts were passed. But these very same people will tell you God <u>still</u> divinely intervenes in Biblical translations today and intervenes in the kingdoms of men today by setting up kings and taking them away. We contend the setting up and taking away of kings and their associated kingdoms of men ended at the same time the *gifted* and *inspired* apostles and those they passed these *gifts* to died or when the *new covenant* came into full force at the destruction of Jerusalem and the tabernacle in A.D. 70. We also contend the need for the inspired word of God ended at this very same time and for the reasons expressed in Jeremiah 31:31-34, Hebrews 8:6-13, and Hebrews 10:15-17, and that God has not divinely intervened in scriptural translations since A.D. 70.

- Jeremiah 31:31-34 – The *new covenant*, as prophesied, would abolish the need for preaching/teaching since God's laws would be put in our inward parts; written in our hearts and we will recognize God as sovereign (sole authority) and He will recognize us as His people

- Hebrews 8:6-13 – The *new covenant,* once established, abolished the need for preaching/teaching since God's laws are NOW written in our hearts and minds. The old covenant was still active, at the time of this writing, but was waxing old and ready to vanish. The old covenant, with its associated laws and ordinances, would remain until the physical tabernacle was destroyed along with the judgment and destruction of Jerusalem (see Hebrews 9:8-11 and Hebrews 2:8) and until a more perfect tabernacle, not made with hands, was established

- Hebrews 10:15-17 – God's *new covenant* was His promise to write His laws in the hearts and minds of man

How many different Bible translations do we have today? Which one is inspired? We contend that none of the 100 or more English Bible translations are inspired, including the KJV.

As of A.D. 70, the so-called divine right of kings and kingdoms of men became inconsequential to those living in the spirit. In essence, the divine right of kings died. The concept of the divine right of kings was never a Godly one, as it was conceived in the mind of man who rejected God as being their sovereign authority.

- I Samuel 8:7 – The people rejected God as their sovereign authority and desired to be ruled by man

God told them, through Samuel, exactly what would happen to them if they persisted in this nonsense. The rejection of God's authority and supreme rule in favor of being ruled by man, leads to bondage. This was <u>not</u> God's plan. Read this revealing account in I Samuel 8:11-20.

- I Samuel 8:11 – Their sons would be taken (enslaved) for the King's personal benefit

- I Samuel 8:12 – Some were to be taken (enslaved) for tilling the King's ground and harvesting the King's crops

- I Samuel 8:13 – Their daughters would be taken (enslaved) to cook for the King

- I Samuel 8:14-15 – Their property would be taken (stolen) and given to the King's servants

- I Samuel 8:16-17 – Their servants would be taken (enslaved) and given to the King's work

- I Samuel 8:18 – The people were told that they would cry out for relief from the tyranny imposed upon them, but that the Lord would ignore their cries

- I Samuel 8:19 – The people ignored Samuel's warnings and showed their preference for being ruled by man rather than being ruled by God

- I Samuel 8:20 – The people envied other kingdoms of men (nations) versus being ruled by God and wanted to be taken care of Nanny State style

We find the same folly and tyranny today when men seek to be ruled over by other men, or women, whether that rule is by monarchy or democracy. Tyranny can come from both forms of rule, but the associated bondage and enslavement begins when people reject God's rule for the preference of being ruled by man.

Actually, the first instance of rejection of God's authority took place in the Garden of Eden. Adam and Eve rejected God's authority when they accepted a pseudo authority (Satan) and believed the lie he promoted that there are no consequences for ignoring God's authority or His truth. In Genesis 3:1-19, we read of the consequences to man and Satan for ignoring God's authority and see God's redemptive plan beginning to unfold.

We later learned Satan ruled over the kingdoms of men (see Matthew 4:8-10). If Satan did not truly have dominion and rule over the kingdoms of men, he could not have offered Christ the possession of them as a temptation. Christ's human element was truly put to the test as the devil did, in fact, have the power to deliver on his offer to Christ.

- Matthew 4:8-10 – Satan offers Christ the kingdoms of the world and their glory if Christ would only fall down and worship him. Christ refused the temptation and said, "…for it is written, thou shalt worship the Lord thy God, and Him only shalt thou serve."

Again, God never intended that man have dominion over man. The following scriptures in Genesis imply that the only thing God intended man to have dominion over was the animal kingdom (Genesis 1:26), the plant kingdom (Genesis 2:15), and their own families and household (Genesis 3:16; 18:18-19).

I do not feel obliged to believe that the same God who has endowed us with sense, reason, and intellect has intended us to forego their use. – **Galileo Galilei**

~

Chapter 5

The END TIMES of the Judaic Age

THE Spirit of the Lord GOD is upon me; because the LORD hath appointed me to preach good tidings unto the meek; he hath sent me to bind up the brokenhearted, to proclaim liberty to the captives, and the opening of the prison to them that are bound; To proclaim the acceptable year of the LORD, and the day of vengeance of our God; to comfort all that mourn; To appoint unto them that mourn in Zion, to give them liberty for ashes, the oil of joy for mourning, the garment of praise for the spirit of heaviness; that they might be called trees of righteousness, the planting of the LORD, that he might be glorified. – **Isaiah 61:1-3**

We will now look at the evolution and completion of God's redemptive plan (prophecy) for dealing with sin and guilt and His plan (prophecy) to restore His *unshared* authority and sovereignty in a kingdom not made with hands.

- Genesis 3:14-15 – Satan's future foretold; through woman's seed, or lineage, Satan's head would be bruised. Satan's seed and woman's seed divided

- I John 3:1-15 – Division of seed (Satan's and God's) expounded upon; pay particular attention to verses 8 and 10, as these verses show clearly God's plan of redemption began moments after the temptation and sin in the Garden of Eden. Cain is described as coming from Satan's seed (evil) and Abel from God's seed (righteous) and <u>love</u> was a distinguishing characteristic between the two

- Matthew 23:29-39 – Satan's lineage portrayed by Christ's chastisement of the scribes and Pharisees

- John 8:33-47 – The Pharisees were of the lineage of Satan who lied (to Eve) from the beginning

- Matthew 13:36-43 – The parable of the tares describing the division and nature of the two seeds (Satan's and the Son of Man); and Judgment

- Acts 13:6-12 – In a time period, *after* the death, burial, and resurrection of Christ, Satan's seed was still active and thriving and Paul (filled with the Holy Ghost) described Elymas as a *child (seed) of the devil* in verse 10

What struck us as fascinating in the above scriptures is the comparison between the *seeds* of good and evil and how this theme continues through the Old and New Testaments. As mere mortals, we cannot choose our physical parents, but as spiritual beings we get to choose our lineage. We can choose evil and pick Satan as our parent or we can choose good and in so doing pick God as our spiritual parent. We can choose to walk in darkness, as Satan's seed, or we can choose to walk in the light as God's seed. We can choose to buy the truth (God, as he is truth; Hebrews 6:17-20) or we can trade God (truth) for the comfort of a lie of which Satan is the father of all (John 8:44). We can choose to walk in the flesh as Satan's seed or walk in the Spirit as God's seed. Again, as reflected in I John 3:8-15, <u>love</u>, or the lack of <u>love</u>, is the distinguishing characteristic between these two lineages.

- Romans 16:20 – Bruising of Satan (under Roman's feet), as an event, *after* the death, burial, and resurrection of Christ and that event would transpire *shortly*. In other words, Christ's death, burial, and resurrection took away the sting of death, but did not <u>yet</u> destroy the kingdoms of the devil and fully establish the *spiritual* kingdom of God (see Luke 21:31-32 referencing the establishment of the kingdom of God after the destruction of Jerusalem, described in Luke 21:20-24, and within their lifetime)

- Luke 21:32 – Christ says <u>all</u> shall be fulfilled within <u>their</u> generation

- Matthew 16:27-28 – Judgment, as an event, would take place in their lifetime

- Matthew 24:34 – Fulfillment of prophecy would take place within their lifetime. This *fulfillment* (of prophecy) would include the judgment (punishment of the Pharisees and Jewish overseers and the reward or rest for those who believed in Christ); Christ's second coming (Luke 21:27); the destruction of Jerusalem and the temple; <u>and</u> the <u>completion</u> of the establishment of the kingdom of God and the ushering in of the *new covenant*

- Revelation 21:3 – Implies a shift would take place whereby the tabernacle of God would no longer be in a centralized location but with man himself (decentralized). Note the similar language in Hebrews 8:10-13, Hebrews 10:16-17, and II Corinthians 6:16

- John 12:31 – Christ said, "<u>Now</u> is *the* judgment of this world" and this statement was made before His death, burial, and resurrection. We need to consider that Christ's death, burial, resurrection, and *the* judgment and dethroning of Satan (Prince of the world) were all closely connected in time

- Hebrews 9:26-28 – References the time frame of <u>now</u> in verse 26. It associates the *end of the world* time frame with Christ's death, burial, and resurrection

Obviously, the phrase *end of the world* or *end of the age* is <u>not</u> describing a future event (from our day and age), but is *more* closely connected to the time frame of Christ's death, burial, and resurrection. The word *world* is translated from the Greek word *aion,* which signifies an *age* or *period of time.* In this particular application, it is broadly referencing the end of the Judaic Age or system of law as signified by Christ's death; the judgment; the second coming of Christ; and the full establishment of the *spiritual* kingdom of God along with the new covenant.

- Galatians 4:3-5 –References a time frame. *Fullness of time* (signifies completion) associated with Christ's redemption of those under the law. [As a side note, those in our dispensation (kingdom of God) have <u>never</u> been under the law]

- I Corinthians 10:1-11 – References a time frame. The admonition was given to not fall for or lust after evil things, as did their predecessors, but learn from their example because the *ends of the world* (judgment) are come

- I John 2:18 – References a time frame. Use of the words *last time* to signify to the generation living <u>then</u> that they were <u>in</u> the *last times.* Also, there were many antichrists present, which signified they were, indeed, in the *last times.* In actuality, the phrase last *time(s)* is translated from the Greek word *hora,* which means hour. As we work our way through the New Testament we can clearly see a shift in how time is referenced. It is a little more laid back in the earlier letters, with the tempo picking up toward the end, as shown here in this passage

- Hebrews 10:36-37 – References a time frame and a promise of reward or rest. The sting of death was removed by the death, burial, and resurrection of Christ, but they were still _eagerly_ looking for their eternal _rest_ with God in heaven (Hebrews 4:1-11) that some of them were promised in their lifetimes (Matthew 16:27-28)

- Matthew 24:1-34 – Some theologians try and split the time frames and events described here. They make the assumption the questions asked by Christ's disciples, in verse 3, were of events separated by thousands of years. But in verses 29-31, where the scripture transitions from describing the fall of Jerusalem to what is commonly referred to as the second coming of Christ, it destroys the false assumption that the second coming of Christ is thousands of years in the future by the use of one word, which is the very first word of verse 29. That word is _immediately_. _Immediately_ after the tribulation (fall of Jerusalem)…verse 30, the Son of man coming in the clouds…verse 31, with a great sound of a trumpet…gathering the elect from the four winds

If _immediately_, in Matthew 24:29, does not mean _immediately_, is there <u>anything</u> we can understand about the Bible? Christ often implied to His disciples that if they wanted to enter heaven, they must become as little children. A child understands what _immediately_ means. If you tell a child he or she can open his or her birthday presents _immediately_, after they blow out the cake candles and open their cards, will they perceive that directive to mean two or three hours later, two or three weeks later, two or three years later, or two thousand years later? Most definitely not! Immediately means immediately. Only an adult can take a simple word like <u>immediately</u> and twist the meaning beyond all recognition in order to support their creed. What's so refreshing about children, and most likely why Christ said to emulate them, is they haven't been so completely and overwhelmingly subdued with _institutional_ creeds that they ignore the obvious.

The concept of <u>all</u> these prophesied events being contained within a short period of time is clearly and consistently stated in parallel accounts in Mark 13:1-27 and Luke 21:5-32. All three accounts more than suggest the fulfillment of <u>all</u> prophecy would take place within their lifetimes. Again, only adults defending *institutional* creeds can twist the meaning of these scriptures beyond all recognition. In these accounts, the people were advised to flee to the mountains from Judea when they observed the abomination of desolation (destruction of Jerusalem) and not dilly-dally around about it. Those upon the rooftops were told not to return and gather their belongings. Those in the fields were told not to retrieve their garments and that flight in the winter, or with children, would be extremely burdensome. There is no way this advisory could apply to anything but the destruction of Jerusalem. To those who believe these scriptures are referring to the end and total destruction of the world and universe, at some future point, we have a question you may want to consider. If the world and universe were going to be totally destroyed, what consolation could be found in fleeing to the mountains? Would not the mountains be destroyed also? Do not these scriptural accounts irrefutably dispel the myth that the destruction of Jerusalem and the judgment or second coming of Christ were going to be separated, in time, by thousands of years?

The best commentary on the Bible is the Bible itself. We want to take a look at the issue of *time* references and see if we can find patterns of Biblical usage that will clarify meaning.

The word *immediately* is translated from the Greek word *Eutheos* and means direct, at once, soon, or shortly. Its usage and meaning can be found and validated in the following scriptures:

- Matthew 4:21-22 – Christ saw James and John mending fishing nets, on the ship, and called to them (v.21), and they *immediately* left the ship and followed Him

- Matthew 8:3 – Christ touched the leper and said be thou clean; and *immediately* his leprosy was cleansed

- Matthew 14:29-31 – Peter began walking on water towards Jesus (v.29) and began to sink (v.30), and Jesus *immediately* stretched forth His hand and saved Peter from sinking

- Mark 2:11-12 – Christ told the bedfast to arise and take up his bed (v.11), and *immediately* (v.12) he arose and took up his bed

- Mark 14:43 – And *immediately*, while Christ was yet speaking, cometh Judas

- Acts 9:17-18 – Ananias told Saul (Paul) that Jesus had arranged for them to meet in order that Paul regain his sight and be filled with the Holy Ghost (v.17), and *immediately* (v.18) the scales fell from his eyes and he regained his sight

- Matthew 24:29-31 – *Immediately* after the tribulation (fall of Jerusalem), the Son of Man will be seen, by man, coming in the clouds (v.30) with the great sound of a trumpet (v.31). (Note: the phrases *coming in the clouds* and *great sound of a trumpet* are those commonly associated with the second coming of Christ)

It's rather obvious the first six scriptural references above did not imply the word *immediately* would be thousands of years into the future. If the scriptures actually mean what they say in those first six references, why would they not signify a similar meaning in the last reference? Can anyone really believe that when Peter began sinking in the sea and Jesus *immediately* stretched forth His hand to save Peter that the time frame for Him performing this life-saving act could have been a couple of hours, days, weeks, years, or possibly two thousand years later? If immediately does not mean immediately, is there <u>anything</u> we can understand about the Bible?

The word *shortly* is translated from the Greek word *Tachos* or *Tacheos* and means briefly, shortly, or quickly. Its usage and meaning can be found and validated in the following scriptures:

- Acts 25:4 – Festus to depart *shortly*
- I Corinthians 4:19 – Paul to come *shortly*
- Philippians 2:19 & 24 – Timotheus and Paul to be sent *shortly*
- II Timothy 4:9 – Paul (death at hand – v.6) requesting Timothy to come *shortly*
- Romans 16:20 – Satan to be bruised *shortly* (death, burial, and resurrection of Christ was obviously not the *end all* to this condition)
- Revelation 1:1 – Revelation of things that must come to pass *shortly*
- Revelation 22:6 – Angel to show the things which must *shortly* be done
- Luke 18:7-8 – God will avenge the elect *speedily*; the word speedily is also translated from the Greek word *tachos*

It's rather obvious the first four scriptural references above did not imply the word *shortly* would be thousands of years into the future. And if the scriptures actually mean what they say in those first four references, why would they not signify a similar meaning in the last four references? Does anyone really believe that when Paul senses his own death being at hand and expresses his desire for Timothy to come *shortly* that he meant for this visit to be two thousand years later? If *shortly* does not mean *shortly*, is there is <u>anything</u> we can understand about the Bible?

The word *quickly* is translated from the Greek word *Tachu* and means shortly, without delay, soon, readily, and quickly. Its usage and meaning can be found and validated in the following scriptures:

- Matthew 5:25 – Agree with thine adversary *quickly*

- Matthew 28:6-8 – Mary and Mary Magdalene went to the empty sepulchre of Jesus, where they were told by the angel that Christ had risen. The angel told them to go *quickly* (v.7) and tell the disciples he is risen. They departed *quickly* and <u>ran</u> to bring the disciples word of Christ's resurrection (v.8)

- John 11:29-31 – She (Mary) arose *quickly* (v.29), and her departure, as witnessed by those Jews comforting her, was described by the words, "she rose up *hastily* and went out…"

- Revelation 22:6-7 – The angel revealing the things which must *shortly* be done (v.6) followed by "Behold, I come *quickly*…"(v.7)

- Revelation 22:12 – "And behold, I come *quickly*…"

- Revelation 22:20 – "…Surely, I come *quickly*."

It's rather obvious the first three scriptural references above did not imply the word *quickly* would be thousands of years into the future. And if the scriptures actually mean what they say in those first three references, why would they not signify a similar meaning in the last three references? To do something *quickly* <u>does not</u> mean two thousand plus years later. If the word *quickly* means two thousand plus years or more, we might as well say the word *quickly* means two million years or more. We contend that the only thing interfering with the meaning of these words is man-made creed. The man-made creed we refer to is what is dispensed by religious institutional *authorities* who, without scriptural basis, declare that Revelation was written after the destruction of Jerusalem and therefore remains a prophecy <u>yet</u> to be fulfilled. This man-made creed takes what Christ died for (our liberty) and returns those who follow it to the bondage of men, kings, kingdoms of men, institutionalism, and Pharisee-ism. This man-made creed spits on the full meaning and significance of Christ's sacrifice. Not only did Christ die that we have hope for eternal life, but he also freed us from *institutional* authority and the associated mischief of *uninspired* and *ungifted* men.

The phrase *at hand* is translated from the Greek word *Eggus* or *Eggizo* and means near, nigh, draw nigh, ready, and to make near. Its usage and meaning can be found and validated in the following scriptures:

- Mark 14:42-43 – Christ said, "let us go; lo, he that betrayeth me is *at hand* (v.42) and *immediately*, while he yet spake, cometh Judas (v.43) (Note: It would appear the words *at hand* and *immediately* convey a similar concept of time)

- John 2:13 – The Passover was *at hand*, and Jesus went to Jerusalem

- John 7:2 – The Jewish feast of the tabernacles was *at hand*

- Romans 13:12 – The night is far spent, the day is *at hand* (What day is Paul referring to here? See v.11)

- Philippians 4:5 – The Lord is *at hand*

- I Peter 4:7 – The end of <u>all</u> things is *at hand*

- Revelation 1:3 – The time is *at hand*

- Revelation 22:10 – The time is *at hand*

It's rather obvious the first three scriptural references above did not imply the phrase *at hand* would be thousands of years into the future. And, if the scriptures actually mean what they say, in those first three references, why would they not signify a similar meaning in the last five references?

One thing is for very certain and that is the phrase *at hand* in no way represents thousands of years as the Bible has plenty of different references to denote longer periods of time than that represented by a person's lifetime of which we will cover momentarily.

The word *nigh* is translated from the Greek word *Eggizo* and means near, nigh, draw nigh, ready, and to make near. Its usage and meaning can be found and validated in the following scriptures:

- Matthew 21:1 – They drew *nigh* unto Jerusalem

- Luke 7:12 – Christ came *nigh* unto the gate of the city

- Luke 19:29 – Christ was come *nigh* to Bethany

- Luke 22:1 – Now the feast of the unleavened bread drew *nigh*

- Acts 10:7-9 – Household servants (v.7) sent to Joppa (v.8) drew *nigh* to the city

- Acts 7:17 – But when the time of the promise drew *nigh*

- Philippians 2:27 – He was sick *nigh* unto death

- Hebrews 7:19 – We draw *nigh* unto God

- James 4:8 – Draw *nigh* to God, and He will draw *nigh* to you

- James 5:8 – For the coming of the Lord draweth *nigh*

It's rather obvious the first nine scriptural references above signified that the word *nigh* meant near in time or space (physical or spiritual) and did not mean, when referencing time, it would be thousands of years into the future. And if the scriptures actually mean what they say in those first nine references, why would they not signify a similar meaning in the last reference?

We can also see Biblical references of *time* that contrast longer periods with shorter periods. We can take a look at the books of Daniel and Revelation, which both foretell the destruction of Jerusalem (see Matthew 24:15) and the *end times* and see the time reference changing from the early days of prophecy to the near fulfillment of that same prophecy. In Daniel 8:19-26, please note the specific use in verse 23 of the phrase *latter time* and in verse 26 the phrase *many days* associated with *the* prophecy. In Revelation 1:3, the phrase *time is at hand* is talking about the same prophecy denoted in Daniel. Note also, in Daniel 8:26, Daniel is told <u>to shut</u> up the vision (prophecy) because it was *many days* in the future versus John being told in Revelation 22:10 to <u>seal not</u> the sayings of the prophecy because the *time is at hand*. Also, in Daniel 12:13, Daniel is told to *rest* until the end of days, when he would receive his lot or reward. In other words, it would be a significant period of time in the future before Daniel would receive his reward at the *end of days* versus what we find in Revelation 22:12, where the angel relays to John that Christ will *come quickly* with his reward. What would be God's purpose in contrasting various different time frames if they had no meaning or significance? Do those who think the Bible is the inspired word of God believe that God minces His words or that he seeks to mislead? Please carefully read Daniel 12:9-13 and Revelation 22:10-12 and ask yourself if these scriptures are not referencing the same event. Revelation is about the *end times* of the Judaic system signified by the life, death, burial, and resurrection of Christ and culminating, in A.D. 70, with the judgment, the destruction of the tabernacle and Jerusalem, <u>and</u> the second coming of Christ. Revelation describes <u>their</u> rapture not ours. Revelation is a prophecy fulfilled, <u>and</u> within their lifetime, as Christ promised.

Now let's take a look at some more parallel accounts of the same events prophesied in both the Old and New Testaments:

- Isaiah 61:1-3 and Luke 4:16-21 – *The day of the Lord's vengeance*

- Joel 2:28-32 and Acts 2:16-21 – *The great and terrible day of the Lord* and *the great and notable day of the Lord* <u>and</u> the *LAST DAYS* (Acts 2:17)

Key wording in Joel 2:28 is, "And it shall come to pass <u>*afterward (last days)*</u>." Acts 2:16-21 actually quotes the prophet, in Joel 2:28-32, and is talking about the same event, and this event is connected to the *last days* (see Acts 2:17).

It also can't be overlooked in Joel 2:28-32 and Acts 2:16-21 of the pouring out of the spirit to be done in the *last days* (see Acts 2:17), which is accounted for and portrayed in the following scriptures:

- Mark 16:14-18 – Christ appeared after His resurrection to the eleven (v.14) and gave them the great commission (v.15). Those who believed and were baptized would be saved, and those who didn't would be damned (v.16), and those who believed would cast out devils, speak with tongues (v.17), take up serpents, drink poison without harm, and heal the sick (v.18)

- I Corinthians 12:1-11 – Concerning spiritual gifts (v.1) no man can say Jesus is Lord, but by the Holy Ghost (v.3), and these gifts are diverse (v.4) and administrated differently but from the same source (v.5). Gifts include wisdom, knowledge (v.8), faith, healing (v.9), working of miracles, prophecy, speaking in tongues, and interpretation of tongues (v.10), and all gifts emanate from the same Spirit (v.11)

- Luke 9:1-2 – Christ gave the twelve disciples power and authority over all devils and gave them the power to heal (v.1) and sent them to preach (limited commission) the kingdom of God and heal the sick (v.2)

- Luke 10:1-20 – Christ gave seventy additional disciples the same powers he gave the twelve (Matthew 10:1-8; Luke 9:1-2). The seventy returned and were astonished at their power over the devils through Christ's name (v.17), and Christ beheld Satan as lightning falling from heaven (v.18), and the disciples were given power to tread on *serpents* and *scorpions* without harm (v.19), but were admonished not to rejoice in this power, but to rejoice because their names are written in heaven

- Acts 10:44-48 – Holy Ghost fell on the hearers of the word, and they spoke in tongues and were baptized

- Revelation 9:1-11 – John saw a star fall from heaven unto the earth and to Him was given the key of the bottomless pit (v.1). There came out of the smoke locusts upon the earth with the power of *scorpions* (v.3) to hurt <u>only</u> those without the seal of God in their foreheads (v.4), but not kill them (v.5) but simply torment them (those without the seal) with the sting of a *scorpion* for five months and to the point they wish they were dead (v.6). The shape of the locusts was like unto horses (v.7), and their tails like unto *scorpions* to hurt men (those without the seal) five months (v.10). And their king was the angel (Satan) of the bottomless pit (v.11)

Please read again, carefully, Luke 10:17-20 and Revelation 9:1-11, and note the same terminology being used to describe Satan's angels. Revelation is about the *end times* of the Judaic system as signified by the life, death, burial, and resurrection of Christ and culminating, in A.D. 70, with the judgment, the destruction of the tabernacle and Jerusalem, <u>and</u> the second coming of Christ. Revelation describes their rapture, not ours. Revelation is a prophecy fulfilled and within their lifetime, as Christ promised.

The very last book of the Old Testament has some interesting tidbits about the judgment upon Jerusalem, as follows:

- Malachi 3:1-5 – The prophecy relating to John the Baptist (the messenger, see Matthew 3:3-12, 11:7-14; Mark 1:2-8; Luke 7:24-28, and 1:13-17) foretold and his preparing the way of the Lord (v.1). Sanctification is depicted by use of the words *refiners fire* and asking who will be able to stand it (v.2-3) and foretelling of the judgment against those who oppress and deceive

- Malachi 4:1-6 – Key passages relating to the coming of John the Baptist and the judgment upon Jerusalem for ignoring the Law of Moses. The righteous shall tread down the wicked in the day the Lord

Now let's take a look at a few New Testament scriptural references that refer to *the end of the world* (age or *aion*):

- Matthew 13:36-40 – The evil seed of Satan or the Wicked One is contrasted with the good seed (children of the kingdom), and the harvest is representing the *end of the world* or Judaic Age and the perverted Judaic system (v.36-39) and the tares are gathered and burned (v.40)

- Matthew 13:49 – ...at the *end of the world* (age); the angels shall separate the wicked from the just

- Matthew 24:1-3 – Question of the disciples regarding the destruction of the temple and the coming of the Lord and the *end of the world (age)*

- Matthew 28:20 – ...and, lo, I am with you always, even unto the <u>*end of the world*</u> (age)

- Hebrews 9:26 – The *end of the world* (age) is associated, in time, with Christ's death

As pointed out earlier, in Hebrews 9:26 we can see Christ's death, burial, and resurrection (sacrifice) took place at the *end of the world* (age). The use of the phrases *end of the world* or *end of the age* is not referencing a future event (from our day and age), but is much more closely connected to the time frame of Christ's death, burial, and resurrection (sacrifice, v.26). Again, the word *world* is translated from the Greek word *aion*, which signifies an *age* or period of time. In this particular application it is broadly referencing the end of the Judaic Age, the old covenant, or system of law, as signified by Christ's death; the judgment; the second coming of Christ; and the establishment of the *spiritual* kingdom of God and the new covenant (Hebrews 8:13). It should be rather obvious, even to the most casual reader, that the phrase *end of the world* did not mean the complete destruction of the earth since almost 2,000 years have gone by since Christ's death (sacrifice, Hebrews 9:26), and the world is still here.

It is of particular importance to note in Hebrews 9:26 the word *world* is used twice, but the Greek words they were each translated from are different. The first use of the word *world* is translated from the Greek word *kosmos* meaning the physical universe or world and its inhabitants, while the second use of the word *world* is translated from the Greek word *aion,* which means <u>age</u>. The KJV (and possibly other translations) use of the word *world* interchangeably, in this instance, greatly distorts and perverts the meaning of the original passage and could lead many people down the dead-*end times* road of believing this passage pertains to the complete destruction of the physical world or universe. As a result, they could mistakenly point to the existence of the physical world today as living proof there is *end times* prophecy yet to be fulfilled. Now is a perfect time to reiterate the fact that the Bible is not the inspired word of God but rather is an *uninspired* human translation of the inspired word of God. There is a vast chasm spanning these two concepts into which many Bible readers have perilously fallen.

To further illustrate our point, take a look at II Peter 3:5-13 in which it states the *world* perished during the flood. Do you really think the *physical world* perished during the flood? Or did the *world*, as it was known to man, perish? If the *physical world* actually perished in the flood, what happened to Noah and his family? If the *world* truly perished during the flood, how come you and I are here? If you believe the heavens and earth that are now kept in store (v.7), that are reserved for destruction again (v.7; Matthew 24:35), and that are to be replaced with a new heaven and earth (v.13) is referring to the *physical world,* wouldn't that require the world to be recreated twice (after the flood and again at judgment)? What we are trying to convey with this exercise is that the *futurist* prediction of the total destruction of the world, as a yet remaining prophecy to be fulfilled, is flawed.

Do you need more proof? In Matthew 24:21, where it describes the fall and destruction of Jerusalem, it indicates the tribulation (fall of Jerusalem) was to be so great there would be nothing of its equal whether considering the past, present, or future. This event represented the total destruction of the Judaic system or world as they knew it, and it was fulfilled, as promised, within the lifetime of many of those who heard Christ speak of it (Matthew 16:28, 24:33-34; Mark 9:1, 13:29-30; Luke 9:27, and Luke 21:31-32).

Now let's take a look at a few New Testament scriptural references that refer to *the end.* The Greek word for *end* is *tello* and means the conclusion of an act or state; termination; or result.

- Matthew 10:22 – ...he that endureth to *the end* shall be saved

- Matthew 24:6 – ...but *the end* is not yet

- I Corinthians 1:8 – Who shall also confirm you to *the end*

- I Corinthians 10:11 – ...and they are written for our admonition, upon whom *the ends* of the world are come

- I Corinthians 15:24 – Then cometh *the end,* when he shall have delivered up the kingdom of God...and put down all rule, authority, and power

- Hebrews 3:6 – ...hold fast the confidence and rejoicing of the hope unto *the end*

- Hebrews 3:14 – ...hold confidence steadfast to *the end*

- Hebrews 6:11 – ...hold diligence commensurate with your hope unto *the end*

- I Peter 4:7 – But *the end* of all things is *at hand*

Matthew 24:6-14 is very interesting, because in answering the questions of the disciples in verse 3 regarding when the temple would be destroyed and the sign of Christ's coming and the *end of the world*, Christ stated in verse 14 that the end will come after the gospel of the kingdom is preached unto all the world. Revelation 11:7-8 confirms that the destruction of Jerusalem (spiritual Sodom) would take place when their preaching was finished. Colossians 1:5-6 and verse 23 suggest the gospel was preached unto the world and to every creature.

In Hebrews 8:6-13 and the parallel account in Jeremiah 31:31-34, it describes the new covenant, yet to come, in which teaching their neighbors would not be necessary because God's laws would be written in their hearts and minds. In Hebrews 8:13, the old covenant was waxing old but not yet vanished because the tabernacle was still standing (see Hebrews 9:8). Keep in mind that the old covenant was waxing old after the death, burial, and resurrection of Christ, but was still active. There was an urgency to preach the gospel unto all the world and to every creature before the end of the Judaic Age came, as signified by the destruction of the tabernacle and Jerusalem and the judgment and second coming of Christ at the *end of the world* (age, Judaic.) I Peter 4:7 reads that the end of *all things* is *at hand* and was an admonishment for them to be watchful. The *all things* is referring to the Judaic Age coming to a close with the destruction of the tabernacle and Jerusalem, and the judgment and second coming of Christ as described in Revelation. It was all part and parcel to the establishment of the new covenant and the kingdom of God as the only God-authorized kingdom (see Revelation 11:15-19). In Daniel 2:34-45, we read of the stone cut out, without hands, smoting the image and becoming a great mountain (power) and filling (through His word) the whole earth, consuming the other kingdoms, and standing forever. In Matthew 21:42-45, this stone is mentioned again with references in verse 44 of breaking and grinding to powder all who resist it. In verse 42 (see Psalms 118:21-23) it refers to the stone the builders rejected. The *builders* were the Jewish Pharisees (religious *authorities*) who would be destroyed at the judgment, along with the destruction of the tabernacle and Jerusalem. There was going to be hell to pay for those who not only rejected the stone (Christ), but vengeance on those who killed the prophets and disciples who preached Christ and the kingdom of God (see Isaiah 28:14-18). The judgment and destruction of Jerusalem (spiritual Sodom) and the tabernacle were the climax to the central Biblical theme that permeates the Old and New Testament. There is only one God. There is only one true authority.

Man rejected God's authority from the very beginning in the Garden of Eden. The first kingdom of man to reject God's authority was Babel, which was the kingdom of Nimrod. Nimrod was described as a mighty one in the earth (Genesis 10:8-10). The Hebrew word for mighty is *gibbor* and means warrior, tyrant, or chief. The kingdom of Babel was later named Babylon and was described as the mother of spiritual harlotry (Jeremiah 3:1-3; Revelation 17:5). God perceived that he was married to His people and considered their turning away from Him as spiritual adultery and idolatry (Jeremiah 3:1-25, 5:7, 31:31-32; Ezekiel chapters 16 and 23). Jerusalem is described as her mother's daughter, implying that Jerusalem was of the spiritual whore lineage of Babylon and quite content, so as can be seen in Ezekiel 16:44-45 and Ezekiel chapter 23. In Ezekiel chapters 16 and 23, we can see Babylon (the mother of spiritual harlotry) had two daughters. One was Jerusalem and the other was Samaria. When we read Revelation 17:5, the key to understanding which nation is being referenced in the female gender is not to focus on Babylon, but her daughters, as depicted in Ezekiel chapters 16 and 23. Jerusalem is the spiritual whore about to be judged (Revelation 17:1) for having committed spiritual fornication with the kings of the earth (Revelation 17:2). The scarlet colored beast Jerusalem was riding, as depicted in Revelation 17:3, was Rome. This whore relationship between Jerusalem and Rome allowed the Jewish religious *authorities* to have Christ crucified so they could preserve their power base. In John 19:15, we can clearly see that the Jewish religious *authorities* (Chief Priests) disavowed God as being their sovereign authority when they made the pronouncement to Pilate that their king was Caesar and demanded of Pilate that Christ be crucified. It is interesting to note the Jewish religious *authorities* could not murder Christ themselves without breaking their own laws (John 18:31), but somehow felt exonerated from their evil deed by co-opting Roman civil *authority* to act in their behalf. Do we not see a similar pattern of behavior today by religious *authorities* and self-described Christians who join with the civil *authorities* as harlots for the purpose of creating global mischief and subsequent opportunities to kill their fellow man? (See Jeremiah 17:5-8 and Isaiah 31:1-3.)

In I Samuel chapter 8, we see the same form of spiritual adultery and idolatry when Israel asked Samuel for a king. God explained to Samuel that the people, in asking for a King, were rejecting God's reign and authority for the preference of being ruled by man (I Samuel 8:7).

When sin entered the world, God not only made a plan for redemption, but He also made plans to restore His authority via a kingdom not made with hands nor of this world (John 18:36; Hebrews 8:1-2, 9:11; Jeremiah 23:5-6, 33:14-18). Christ's disciples were confused on this very issue, as many still are today. His disciples were looking for an earthly kingdom and many today are looking for the same thing. Both have missed the spiritual boat. A kingdom is simply a territory. God's kingdom is a spiritual territory not made with hands (John 18:36). Our souls are part of that kingdom if we accept God as our sole authority. We can look around today and see many kingdoms of men and make the ignorant declaration that <u>all</u> prophecy hasn't been fulfilled because of the still-remaining kingdoms of men. We need to re-read John 18:36 and ask ourselves why we continually attempt to deceive ourselves by comparing apples (physical kingdoms made with hands) to oranges (spiritual kingdoms not made with hands). God's kingdom is not of this world because of the sinful nature of man. Throughout history there is nothing that man touches that isn't eventually perverted to evil ends.

The only way the kingdom of God could forever reign in this world of <u>freewill</u> was to make it spiritual in nature. Otherwise, the *authorities* in the political and religious *institutional* realm would hijack it and supplant it with their worship of *institutionalism* (spiritual idolatry).

Please read carefully John 6:14-68 to see just how thick-headed those people were that Christ was attempting to reach. They could not see the forest (spiritual) for the trees (physical). When they saw His miracles (v.14), he perceived they wanted to make Him a *physical* king (v.15), and Christ disappeared into the mountain and later to Capernaum via a ship. These same carnally minded people went seeking Him again in Capernaum (v.24), and when they caught up with Him were heavily chastised for thinking in *physical* terms (v.26-27), i.e., full bellies. They were still thinking in *physical* terms when thinking back on Moses and manna in the wilderness filling the bellies of their fathers (v.30-31). They began murmuring against Jesus (v.41) in response to Him telling them He was the bread of life (eternal), sent from God (v.38-39), that would satisfy their <u>spiritual</u> hunger (v.35). This murmuring was based, again, on their *physical* association or observation they had of His parents, Mary and Joseph (v.42). Christ responded (v.49-58) by telling them their fathers who ate manna (physical food) in the wilderness were now dead. Christ offered them spiritual manna for eternal life. Some of the disciples were disbelieving (v.60), and Christ knew it from the beginning (v.64). Those disciples left Christ (v.66) because they were looking for a *physical* kingdom of God wherein they would have full *physical* bellies and power. Christ told them (v.63) that the *physical* (flesh) profited nothing, but that His words are spiritual and offer life (eternal). After these disciples left, he went to the twelve apostles and asked them if they, too, were going to leave (v.67).

Physical kingdoms of men are as temporal as our physical bodies. They simply come and go…one after another and turn to dust. No longer, after A.D. 70, does God use kingdoms of men to accomplish His work. His work was completed with the establishment of the kingdom of God and the second covenant (Hebrews 8:10-13).

Today, we are continually deceived by those who proclaim the Biblical accounts were written to us and for our benefit. We would contend that when Christ told the disciples that <u>all</u> prophecy would be fulfilled within their lifetime, He was talking to them and for them, alone, because of the urgent nature of His message. This was not simply a message of salvation, but also of the judgment and destruction of Jerusalem, the destruction of the tabernacle, and the full establishment of the kingdom of God, along with the fulfillment of the promise of the second covenant. This was a monumental event of enormous magnitude. It was the passing of the old (*physical*) and the bringing in of the kingdom of God (*spiritual*). At that point in time, kingdoms of men became inconsequential to those who think in spiritual terms. Men, as fitting to their nature, began re-establishing themselves as *authorities* in the religious and political world, and the people soon began to willingly give up their liberty for a yoke of bondage.

Many of us are no different today. Many still clamor for kings and spiritual *authorities* (shepherds) who will speak to them smooth things (Isaiah 30:8-13), and who falsely promise to protect them from the consequences and realities of their ill-formed beliefs, decisions, and actions.

Now, let's take a look at a few New Testament scriptural references that refer to *the last/latter times, days,* etc.

- I Timothy 4:1-3 – ...in *the latter times* some shall depart from the faith (v.1) searing their conscience with a hot iron (v.2) forbidding to marry, and commanding to abstain from meats (v.3)

- II Timothy 3:1 – ...in *the last days* perilous times shall come

- Hebrews 1:2 – Hath in *these last days* spoken to us by His Son

- I Peter 1:5 – ...ready to be revealed in *the last time*

- I Peter 1:20 – ...but was manifest in *these last times* for you

- II Peter 3:3-4 – ...there shall come in *the last days* scoffers

- I John 2:18 – Little children, it is *the last time* (hour): and as ye have heard that antichrist shall come, even <u>now</u> are there many antichrists; whereby we <u>know</u> that it is *the last time* (hour). (A couple of questions to the *futurists*: What about this passage don't you understand? If denying Christ's first coming <u>then</u> made one an antichrist (II John 7), what does that make those <u>today</u> who deny Christ's second coming as being a past event?)

These scriptural references applied to the Judaic Age. The Judaic Age was the world (time or age) in which they lived, and it was quickly coming to a close, with much fanfare. It was not an insignificant event, because the bringing to fulfillment the kingdom of God and new covenant was what man had been anxiously anticipating for thousands of years. There were also those waiting since the beginning of time in Hades and figuratively under the altar for not only their judgment, but also their vindication (Revelation 6:9-10 and Luke 18:7-8). In other words, the above bulleted scriptures meant exactly what they said. It was <u>the</u> last times and very imminent for those it was written to.

It is sometimes difficult for modern-day churchgoers to fully appreciate the profanity of those Jewish religious leaders, overseers, shepherds, priests, and false prophets (Pharisees and scribes) who persecuted and killed God's prophets, Christ, and Christ's disciples. Modern-day preachers, pastors, elders, and deacons really don't like to talk about it too much because of the natural conclusions that might be taken away from such a discussion. To better appreciate the intense profanity of those spiritual leaders during that time frame, and why the destruction of Jerusalem was so critical to re-establishing and restoring God's sovereignty and balancing the scales of justice, read Ezekiel 34; Jeremiah 6:13-15, 22:22, 23:1-6, 23:14-40; Zechariah 11; Malachi 2:1-4:6; Matthew 15:12-14, 23:1-39; John 11:47-53, 12:42-43; and Acts 4:8-21, 24:1-9. Yes, Christ came to save the lost, but he also came to judge and destroy the wickedness going on in Jerusalem, which was called spiritual Sodom. And this judgment wasn't going to be 2,000 or more years into the future. God was longsuffering enough towards these people waiting as long as he did, and His sense of justice towards those faithful ones waiting under the altar and to His only Son who died a most cruel death was not going to be delayed any longer. Jerusalem was judged and destroyed in A.D. 70, along with the temple and tabernacle. Those faithful ones under the altar (Revelation 6:9-11) were finally vindicated when their persecutors were judged and thrown into the lake of fire. Christ presided over this judgment and destruction. The Old Law, at that point in time, was transformed, and the new covenant and *spiritual* kingdom of God came into full play. All scripture was fulfilled at this time, thereby making the rapture a past event. Those were truly the last times of the Judaic system, which was the world as the Jew knew it to be. The errant Judaic world was destroyed. The evilness associated with the Judaic world was the haughty, abusive, and controlling nature of the Jewish religious leaders. Why would God deliver His flock from these evil leaders (Ezekiel 34:10) and the Judaic system only to give His treasured flock back to mere mortals (pastors, elders, bishops, and deacons) to preside over indefinitely?

During the 40-year Christian dispensation, overseers (elders and deacons) were in congregations, but they were *gifted*, via the Holy Ghost, and could heal, cast out devils, speak in tongues, prophesy, and interpret. They were also divinely appointed to those positions of leadership. Has something of a miraculous nature happened to man that would somehow make our modern-day spiritual leaders better than those spiritual leaders God destroyed in A.D. 70? Those spiritual leaders God destroyed in A.D. 70 and their modern-day counterparts have something in common. Neither group had, or has, the *gift* of the Holy Ghost to heal, cast out devils, speak in tongues, prophesy truthfully, or interpret accurately. Without these unique *gifts*, we are all just mere mortals subject to the frailties of man and severely challenged in spiritually leading ourselves, much less pretending to lead others.

Many pooh-pooh the significance of the destruction of Jerusalem and believe this is just one more insignificant city destroyed by God among many cities destroyed prior to this time and many cities to be destroyed in the future. We have zero evidence God is working in this fashion today. Few, today, make the claim God has talked to them from a burning bush, a stationary cloud or through an angel, but they ironically attribute the *institutional* murder and mayhem around the globe as the work of God. Where is the evidence God is working through the kingdom of men and for what purpose that hasn't already been achieved? The great commission was fulfilled prior to the destruction of Jerusalem and individuals born after this event are in a different dispensation whereby God's laws are written in their hearts. His kingdom (spiritual) has been established in such a way that man can't corrupt it. *Gifted* men no longer exist, because the need to preach the gospel of the kingdom has ceased. A lot of work had to be done in a relatively short period of time, and it was completed in A.D. 70.

Now let's take a look at a few New Testament scriptural references that refer to *the day, that day, the last days, the day of the Lord, the day of God, the great day,* and *that great and notable day of the Lord*:

- Matthew 25:13 – ...for ye know not *the day* nor the hour wherein the Son of man cometh

- Luke 17:30-31 – ...thus shall it be in *the day* when the Son of man be revealed (v.30). In *that day*, he which shall be upon the housetop (v.31)...

- Romans 2:14-29 – The Gentiles did by nature what the Jews were given laws to do (v.14), but failed miserably in actually carrying them out in their own lives (v.19-21). The Jews talked it but did not walk it and in doing so blasphemed the name of God (v.23-24). A real Jew, or chosen one of God, is one who focuses not on outward manifestations (*physical*) but inward things (*spiritual*) of the heart (v.29; see also Jeremiah 4:4). In *the day* when God shall judge the secrets (of the heart) of men by Jesus Christ according to my gospel (v.16)

- Hebrews 10:23-25 – hold fast the profession of our faith (v.23) and provoke unto love and good works (v.24). Not avoiding each other, but exhorting each other as ye see *the day* approaching (v.25)

- Matthew 7:22 – Many will say to me in *that day*, have we not prophesied, cast out devils, and in thy name done many wonderful works?

- Matthew 24:36 – But of *that day* and hour knoweth no man

- Luke 21:34 – Take heed, lest ye become consumed with the world and *that day* takes you by surprise

- I Thessalonians 5:4-6 – But, ye are not in darkness and beware *that day* not overtake you as a thief (v.4). You are not of darkness, but of light (v.5). Therefore don't sleep, as one in the dark, but watch and be sober (v.6)

- II Thessalonians 2:3-4 – Don't be deceived by <u>man</u>, for *that day* shall not come, except there come a falling away first, and that man of sin be revealed, the son of perdition (v.3); Who opposeth and exalteth himself above all that is called God, or that is worshipped; so that he as God sitteth in the temple of God, showing himself that he is God (v.4)

- II Timothy 1:12 – …for I know whom I have believed, and am persuaded that he is able to keep that which I've entrusted unto him against *that day*

- II Timothy 4:8 – …the righteous judge shall give me a crown at *that day*

- I Corinthians 1:7-8 – So that you not be disappointed; waiting for the coming of our Lord Jesus Christ: who shall sustain you to the end, that you may be blameless in *the day* of our Lord Jesus Christ

- I Corinthians 5:5 – Deliver the fornicator (v.1) to Satan (i.e., separate yourselves from him) so that he might ultimately be saved in *the day* of the Lord Jesus

- II Corinthians 1:14 – …mutual rejoicing in *the day* of the Lord Jesus

- Philippians 2:16 – Holding forth the word of life (eternal) that I may rejoice in *the day* of Christ

- I Thessalonians 5:2 – For yourselves know perfectly that *the day* of the Lord so cometh as a thief in the night

- II Peter 3:8-15 – To the scoffers, who were impatiently waiting for Christ's second coming, Peter explains… But, beloved, be not ignorant of this one thing, that one day is with the Lord as a thousand years, and a thousand years as one day (v.8) and is not slack when it concerns His promise and longsuffering nature (v.9). But *the day* of the Lord will come as a thief in the night; in which the heavens shall pass away with a great noise, and the elements shall melt with fervent heat, the earth also and the works that are therein shall be burned up (v.10). Considering this destruction, what manner of persons should you then be (v.11-12)? We look with great expectation for a new heaven and a new earth, wherein dwelleth righteousness (v.13) therefore be diligent and blameless (v.14). And recognize that the longsuffering the Lord is extending others is the same longsuffering he extended you for the purpose of salvation

[Important note: The above passage is often taken out of context as it pertains to the phraseology *one day is with the Lord as a thousand years, and a thousand years as one day* and is often used to denote that we can never understand any time references as being definitive. Not so. Verse 9 implies that the Lord is not slack concerning His promise as some men perceive because of their impatience and self-centered nature. We contend that if a thousand years had gone by before they received their promise, it would have represented slackness on God's part. The key to understanding this passage is in referencing a Greek dictionary. *A thousand* is translated from the Greek word *chilioi* which means a plural of uncertain relation. Contrast this with one, two, or three thousand which <u>is</u> definitive. *One thousand* is translated from the Greek word *chilias* and means <u>one</u> thousand. So, the usage of <u>a</u> thousand in this passage is simply for the purpose of expressing God's longsuffering nature and love...nothing more, nothing less. To put this in a more complete context we can turn to I Peter 4:7, and we see that *the end of all things is at hand* and that these things would be fulfilled within the lifetimes of those he was speaking to, as stated in Matthew 24:34 and elsewhere. The end of <u>all</u> things includes <u>all</u> prophecy.]

- Acts 2:16-21 – ...as prophesied by Joel (v.16), it shall come to pass in *the last days,* saith God, I will pour out my Spirit upon all flesh: and your sons and daughters shall prophesy, and your young men shall see visions, and your old men shall dream dreams (v.17): His servants and handmaidens would receive this Spirit and prophesy (v.18): and wonders and signs in heaven and earth to include blood, fire, and vapour of smoke (v.19): the sun will be turned to darkness and the moon to blood, before *that great and notable day of the Lord* (v.20): and it shall come to pass, that whomsoever shall call on the name of the Lord shall be saved

- Jude 1:6 – And the unfaithful angels who deserted God are kept bound in everlasting chains in darkness unto the judgment of *the great day*

- Revelation 6:15-17 – And the kings of the earth, and the great men, and the rich men, and the chief captains, and the mighty men, and every bondman, and every free man, hid themselves in the dens and in the rocks of the mountains (v.15); and they begged the mountains to fall on them to hide them from God and the wrath of the Lamb (v.16): For *the great day* of His wrath is come; and who shall be able to stand?

- Revelation 16:14 – For they are the spirits of devils, working miracles, which go forth unto the kings of the earth and the whole world, to gather them to the battle of *that great day* of God Almighty

Acts 2:16-21 above is referring to that period of time when the gospel was being preached unto all the world and every creature, but prior to the judgment, the destruction of the tabernacle and Jerusalem, and the ushering in of the new covenant which could <u>not</u> be in force while the tabernacle was still standing (Hebrews 9:8). We see in verse 17 that this period of time was referred to as the LAST DAYS.

Now let's take a look at a few New Testament scriptural references referring to *the day of wrath, the Day of Judgment, the day of redemption, the time of thy visitation, the year of their visitation,* and *the last day*:

- Romans 2:5 – But thy hardness of heart will lay up treasures of wrath that God will return to you in *the day of (His) wrath* and judgment

- Matthew 10:15 – ...It shall be more tolerable for the land of Sodom and Gomorrah in *the day of judgment*, than for that city

- Matthew 12:36 – But I say unto you, That every idle word that men shall speak, they shall give account thereof in *the day of judgment*

- II Peter 3:7 – But the heavens and the earth, which are now, by the same word are kept in store, reserved unto fire against *the day of judgment* and perdition of ungodly men

- I John 4:16-17 – And we have known and believed the love that God hath to us. God is love; and he that dwelleth in love dwelleth in God, and God in him (v.16). Herein is our love made perfect, that we may have boldness in *the day of judgment*: because as he is, so are we in this world

- Ephesians 4:30 – And grieve not the holy Spirit of God, whereby ye are sealed unto *the day of redemption*

- Luke 19:41-44 – He (Christ) beheld the city and wept over it (v.41). Your spiritual blindness cost you the peace that was rightly yours (v.42). Your enemies (the Romans) will cast a trench around you and pin you down from every side to leave you no escape (v.43; see Revelation 20:9; Luke 21:20). They will flatten you, your children, and your buildings to the ground because you didn't know *the time of thy visitation*

- Jeremiah 23:10-12 – For the land is full of adulterers (spiritual) and their land is no longer fruitful (v.10). The prophet and the priest are profane and wicked (v.11). They are on the slippery slope to the dark place and will fall in because God will bring evil upon them in *the year of their visitation*

- John 6:39-40 – And this is the Father's will which hath sent me, that of all which he hath given me I should lose nothing, but should raise it up again at *the last day* (v.39). And this is the will of him that sent me, that every one which seeth the Son, and believeth on him, may have everlasting life: and I will raise him up at *the last day* (v.40)

- John 6:54 – Whoso eateth my flesh, and drinketh my blood, hath eternal life; and I will raise him up at *the last day*

Many scriptures suggested, to their hearers, a tone of urgency and immediacy beyond that which can logically be applied to us today. Today, preachers often speak about the lack of urgency in attitudes towards things spiritual without realizing the distortion of scripture and the twisting of the meaning of words to make these specific verses apply today thousands of years after they were written and possibly thousands upon thousands of years into the future actually contributes to the lethargy and the heavy eyelids occupying pews.

From a personal standpoint, of course, we don't know when we will die. But the scriptural discussions above in which time references were involved discount the issue of physical death and were applied to a more broad consideration of *the day* approaching in which their salvation and reward would be fully realized and the realization it would take place within some of their lifetimes (see Matthew 16:28; Mark 9:1; and Luke 9:27). Those who were older and died before *the day* was fulfilled knew absolutely they would not be waiting long before their own resurrection, judgment, and reward would be realized.

The sense of urgency by the early Christians was naturally manifested because of the significance of *the times* and dispensation they were living in and the historical and spiritual significance of the prophecy being fulfilled and completed at that time. They knew Old Testament scripture much better than we know our Bibles. This same sense of urgency doesn't equate with the dispensation we are living in today, and to force or unnaturally duplicate it by pounding the pulpit and making it so is as pointless as attempting to drive a square peg into a round hole. When one's home is on fire, the sense of urgency to escape the carnage is not fabricated, but is very real. Likewise, when the end of the Judaic Age was imminent, the sense of urgency to escape the carnage needed no fabrication but was very real.

Many *uninspired* evangelists preach constantly about the *end times* pointing to this or that event as signifying *those days* are upon us and attempt to use fear as a tool to motivate their listeners without realizing that all throughout our age there have been events or happenings taking place that could equally signify the *end times*. This folly has been going on for a long, long, time. We can see that in Matthew 24:21-22, Mark 13:19, and Jeremiah 30:7-9, this period, which few dispute pertains to the destruction and fall of Jerusalem, was of such significance that it would never be equaled in the future. Daniel 12:1-2 describes the same event but adds a very interesting tidbit when it mentions the deliverance of God's people (those found written in the book –verse 1) and the resurrection of the dead in verse 2, more commonly associated with Christ's second coming.

If the calamity associated with the judgment and destruction of Jerusalem has no equal in the past, present, or future, does that not let a bit of air out of the futurist's *end times* calamity balloon? How many of us would not agree that a calamity involving continuous rain for 40 days and nights whereby the entire earth was covered with water, to include the highest mountains and where all life (except those in the ark) was destroyed, was a significant event in the history of mankind? According to Matthew 24:21-22, Mark 13:19, and Jeremiah 30:7-9, the calamity associated with the coming destruction of Jerusalem is described, by necessary inference, as being <u>more</u> significant than the calamity associated with the flood in Noah's day. The calamity associated with the judgment and destruction of Jerusalem was, is, and forever will be, unparalleled. If someone is waiting around in anticipation of a greater calamity, according to these scriptures, they are going to be sorely disappointed.

So, the *end times* many are looking for today pale in comparison to what took place in A.D. 70 and in our view is simply a mirage, or an illusion, because the *end times* (Judaic Age, its judgment and destruction, second coming of Christ, and ushering in of salvation and the new covenant), as portrayed in scripture, are past events. There are no other *end times* other than our own physical death and immediate judgment.

Still not convinced? Turn to Matthew 5:17-18. Verse 18 implies that the law will not pass away until <u>all</u> is fulfilled. This scripture raises a very important and critical question. If <u>all</u> prophecy (to include the judgment and second coming of Christ) is not yet fulfilled, would not the Old Law still be in force for those who were not yet converted to Christ? The Old Law required a tabernacle for animal sacrifices, did it not? If not one jot or tittle was to pass from the law till <u>all</u> was fulfilled, would not the tabernacle be a critical component of the Old Law that would still be in force for those yet to be converted? With the tabernacle missing in action, it would appear more than a jot or tittle of the Old Law has indeed passed away. If one is to believe Matthew 5:17-18 is the inspired word of God, the only conclusion that can be drawn is that <u>all</u> prophecy has been fulfilled, and the rapture and the associated *end times* are a matter of history.

It may be difficult for some to accept the fact the spiritual world does not revolve around <u>their</u> present generation. It may be attributable to our centrist nature which wants to believe we are at the center point, or balance point, of a linear line in history that includes the past, present, and future. The closing out of the Judaic World and the ushering in of the kingdom and new covenant, Christ's second coming, the judgment, and the destruction of the tabernacle and Jerusalem, in A.D. 70, actually represents the center point in spiritual history where God's sovereignty and absolute *spiritual* rule was restored. His rule is the <u>only</u> authorized rule to those whom he calls His children and also to those who recognize Him as their God.

And he came to Nazareth, where he had been brought up: and, as his custom was, he went into the synagogue on the sabbath day, and stood up for to read. And there was delivered unto him the book of the prophet Esaias. And when he had opened the book, he found the place where it was written, The Spirit of the Lord is upon me, because he hath anointed me to preach the gospel to the poor; he hath sent me to heal the brokenhearted, to preach deliverance to the captives, and recovering of sight to the blind, to set at liberty them that are bruised, To preach the acceptable year of the Lord. And he closed the book, and he gave it again to the minister, and sat down. And the eyes of all them that were in the synagogue were fastened on him. And he began to say unto them, This day is this scripture fulfilled in your ears. – **Luke 4:16-21**

~

Chapter 6

What's Wrong with the Congregational Church Model?

Just as the *institutional* chief priests, Pharisees, and Sadducees rejected Christ, has *institutionalism* today rejected the kingdom of God for an inferior "church club" substitute that attempts to replicate a structure and form of the original but absent divine intervention (miraculous healing, raising of the dead, casting out of devils, speaking in tongues, etc.) and <u>purpose</u>?

The apostles had a mandate (preaching Christ crucified and the kingdom) that no longer applies today. The kingdom has already come, and we are partakers of that new covenant if we so choose. The new covenant is that condition wherein God has written His laws in our hearts and minds and, by our choice, he is to us a God, and we are to Him a people. People can still choose to reject God as their sovereign authority, but it doesn't alter the fact of His sovereignty because His kingdom is a *spiritual* kingdom not made with human hands nor capable of being corrupted by human hands. If we reject God's sovereignty for the preference of *institutionalism*, we reject the kingdom of God along with our spiritual nature, and choose an inferior *fleshly* substitute. We manifest who our sovereign authority is by our conduct.

During our journey on this earth, we can either choose to believe we are human beings having a spiritual experience (the *institutional* model), or we can choose to believe we are spiritual beings having a human experience (the kingdom of God model). It is this distinction between a predominantly *flesh*-oriented existence juxtaposed to a predominantly *spirit*-oriented existence that's at the core of Christ's teachings.

If we choose to believe we are human beings having a spiritual experience on this earth, we are predominantly *flesh*-oriented. If we choose to believe we are spiritual beings having a human experience, on this earth, we are predominantly *spirit*-oriented. This distinction may seem trite to some, but for us this distinction is crucial in accepting the liberty we believe to be our birthright. Ironically, we've found that the more *spirit*-oriented we are, versus *flesh*-oriented, the more liberty we have during our human experience. The *flesh*, because it is temporal in nature, doesn't have the hold on us it once did, and therefore the coercive brokers of such items don't have as much leverage over our behavior. The *flesh* brokers (kingdoms of men) desire to use the tools of force and fraud to perpetuate dependency, scarcity, and tyranny over mankind, while God's kingdom fosters the exact opposite condition of liberty, abundance, equality, and justice. When viewing our lives as simply a short human experience on this earth, it contrasts the temporal with the eternal, and our choices begin to naturally reflect our spiritual priorities rather than those *fleshly* priorities highly esteemed by men (Luke 16:15; James 4:1-4; Matthew 6:24). When we let the expectations of men and *institutions* of men shape our belief system, we become their bondservants.

For the first 40 years of our lives, we fell in the *institutional* camp of being *flesh*-oriented because we were born into a flawed belief system and were a little slow in recognizing and resolving the bondage associated with that belief system.

The *institutional* model is *flesh*-oriented and patterned after the old Judaic system of doing things by rote that was destroyed in A.D. 70. The kingdom of God model, on the other hand, is *spiritual* in nature where the focus is on matters of the heart and love rather than rituals that are, more often than not, devoid of love.

The congregational church model, as depicted in the New Testament, was a temporary tool allowing those under the law (*physical*) to transition away from a system that was in the process of vanishing away. The congregational model served as an interim measure for those under the law until the kingdom of God was fully established in A.D. 70, with the judgment and destruction of Jerusalem along with the destruction of the temple and tabernacle.

The congregational model served as an interim measure for those coming out of the old law (Galatians 4:3-5) who had accepted Christ's blood as atonement for their sins instead of the traditional model of offering animal sacrifices under the soon-to-be-terminated Judaic system. Anyone born after A.D. 70 has never been under the old law so the congregational model no longer applies. If the congregational model had been designed to be a permanent fixture, there would, by necessity, still be healing, casting out of devils, and speaking in tongues to distinguish the true prophets from the false prophets.

Even in the Christian dispensation when the apostles and disciples were *gifted* with the Holy Ghost and could speak in tongues, heal the sick, and cast out evil spirits...corruption was prevalent (Acts 20:28-30; I John 2:18-19; II Peter 2:1-3; Galatians 1:6-9; and II Peter 3:16-17). How much more corruption and imperfection and straying from the truth is there when these types of *gifts* are not prevalent? And by what authority do *uninspired* and *ungifted* men today attempt to replicate that which is impossible to replicate?

There is no scriptural authority for "church clubs" unless they can be replicated precisely and completely to the New Testament pattern. Until they can convincingly heal, raise the dead, cast out devils, prophesy, speak in tongues, and interpret, as done in the New Testament model, they are simply play acting, much like those adults who don Civil War costumes and perform re-enactments of famous Civil War battles in which they fire blanks at each other instead of real bullets and cannon balls. The major difference between the two types of re-enactments is that the Civil War aficionados fully realize what they are doing is a re-enactment, while the "church clubs" are convinced their activities are a genuine continuation of the original New Testament congregational model, even if they happen to be missing a significant number of *divine* ingredients.

Fortunately, in the kingdom of God and under the new covenant, what we need to know is written in our hearts and minds. For those who believe the Bible is the inspired word of God, they can turn again to Hebrews 8:6-13 and Hebrews 10:16-17 and find out about the new covenant.

For some strange reason, it will be a tremendous test of faith, for some calling themselves Christians, to consider that the God who created the heavens and the earth in six days might be capable of writing His law in our hearts and minds. They would rather recklessly believe God left it in the hands of the political and religious *authorities*. God did that once, and the political and religious *authorities*, in true conspiratorial fashion, crucified His Son. We, in turn, crucify God's Son when we show our preference, loyalty, and allegiance to *institutions* attempting to play the role of Nanny State caretaker over our physical and/or spiritual well-being.

Is uniformity attainable? Millions of innocent men, women, and children, since the foundation of Christianity, have been burnt, tortured, fined, and imprisoned; yet we have advanced not one inch towards uniformity. What has been the effect of coercion? To make one half of the world fools and the other half hypocrites. – **Thomas Jefferson**

~

Chapter 7

Who Am I, What Am I Doing Here?

Many beginning to possibly question the *institutional* creeds they've inherited and who are also beginning to question the man-conceived creed of the second coming of Christ as being a *future* event may now logically be pondering over our mission and purpose on this earth and also questioning what God wrote in our hearts and minds.

If we are no longer required to go unto the world and preach the gospel; if we are no longer required to attend *institutional* meeting places; and if we are no longer required to participate in the various *institutionally* mandated programs that show our allegiance to the *institution* and those who preside over it, what is our mission or purpose in life? Is our purpose simply to act as a passage for food (Philippians 3:19), or is something else required?

Are we paying attention to what is written in our hearts, or do we ignore it for a less perfect *uninspired* and *ungifted* institutional model that tends to choke out genuine and spontaneous love, for inferior work programs that someone presides over with a clipboard or peg board? Have we let the *institutional* precepts of *uninspired* and *ungifted* men blot out the writing that God has placed in each of our hearts? Are we too busy sucking wind and going nowhere on the *institutional* hamster wheel to see our plight? Is too much of our precious time being taken up with *institutional* processes and maintenance schemes that resemble the burdensome Judaic rituals and customs Christ came to liberate us from? Are we straining on Pharisee-ism and gnats and swallowing camels?

Do we need to do as Christ suggests and become like little children or do we remain in our *institutionalized* adult states with a seared over conscience whereby we continue twisting words and scripture a child can easily understand beyond all recognition? Do we continue clutching and cleaving to the security of what is familiar but to also that which enslaves us, or do we embrace the liberty Christ freely shed His blood for?

So, what is it that God has written in our hearts? Maybe we need to look into the eyes of a baby or small child and reflect on what is so very evident. Do we see the reflection of God and His love for us in those innocent eyes, or are we too busy to notice?

Could love, the one ingredient the world is sorely lacking, possibly be our sole (soul's) purpose on this earth? *Institutionalism* can easily choke the life and love out of each of us. Some can possibly love in spite of these *institutional* shackles, but why would anyone knowingly carry all that dead weight around? Would it not be preferential to put the wind at our backs and under our wings instead of choosing a course directly in the path of *institutional* storms and mischief whereby we experience downdrafts and headwinds that could easily cost us our souls while experiencing a life of bondage and calamity during our short journey on this earth? We have religious *institutionalism* on almost every street corner and so little love. Hmmm. There has to be a message in there somewhere.

The message of the religious *authorities* is usually not love, but rather obedience. What obedience are they talking about? Are they talking about the plan of salvation? Are they talking about the order of worship? Are they talking about instrumental music? Are they talking about sprinkling versus immersion? Are they talking about not forsaking the assembling of the saints? Are they talking about the *authority* of the elders? Are they talking about tithing or giving as one has been prospered? Are they talking about the Great Commission? Yes, these are predominant themes in religious *institutions* because their very survival depends upon them. Their position on these issues is what separates them from others and makes them unique. It becomes their brand or flag for their followers to rally around.

Well, what was Christ's response to the question of commandments and obedience in Matthew 22:35-40?

- Matthew 22:35-40 – A lawyer (v.35) asks Christ (v.36) which is the great commandment in the law? Jesus responded, Thou shalt love the Lord thy God with all thy heart, and with all thy soul, and with all thy mind (v.37). This is the first and great commandment (v.38). And the second is like unto it, Thou shalt love thy neighbor as thyself (v.39). On these two commandments hang all the law and the prophets (v.40).

On these two commandments above hang all the law and the prophets. What do you think this means? If we take a look at Exodus 20:1-17, we can find what is commonly referred to as the Ten Commandments, which is the law Christ was referring to in Matthew. If we divide these commandments roughly in half, we can see the first portion of the commandments deal with our relationship to our Heavenly Father, and the second half of these commandments deal with our relationship to our fellow man. We can clearly see love is at the very core of these commandments (see Romans 13:8-10). If we love God with all our heart, mind, and soul, we will refrain from showing allegiance and loyalty to idols and idolatrous *institutions*. If we love our neighbor as ourselves, we won't be killing them, committing adultery with their spouses, stealing from them, bearing false witness, or coveting their <u>oil</u>. Love is truly at the core of the Ten Commandments but was not truly manifested in the hearts of those it was given to (Matthew 15:1-20). The heart is basically our conscience. God's new covenant promise was to write His laws upon our hearts and minds (Hebrews 8:6-13, 10:16-17; and Jeremiah 31:31-34).

In Romans 1:16-2:16 Paul very succinctly explains this whole idea about conscience, the heart, and how *institutionalism* chokes and stifles the very essence of our mission on this earth. Paul says, in writing to the Romans, that the gospel is for everyone to include the Jews and the Greeks (v.16). The gospel portrays the righteousness (*justice* translated from the Greek word *dikaiosune*) of God and that those that are *just* live by faith (v.17). The judgment and wrath of God will befall the ungodly and unrighteous (*unjust*) who hold (*spout*) truth while living contrary to it and *unjustly* (v.18). These ungodly and unjust individuals have no excuse because God has manifested His deity, omnipotence, sovereignty, and eternal nature to them via the creation of the universe and the wonders it contains (v.19-20). They refused to glorify God in spite of the evidence and became unthankful fools with a heart devoid of light (v.21-22). They changed the glory of God to a *lesser* image (idolatry, *institutionalism*, and denominationalism), as a corruptible and pseudo substitute for the <u>real deal</u> (v.23). God turned His back on them (v.24) because they sold the truth and bought a lie and worshipped their *institutions* and inferior idolatrous substitutes (v.25). God turned His back on them (v.26-27) to receive their due recompense (consequences) for removing Him (God) from their conscience (heart) and rejecting Him (God) as the one and only true sovereign authority (v.28-32). In chapter 2 Paul compares the justice of God to the justice of man and finds man severely wanting because God judges according to truth and with the ability to see into a man's heart (I Samuel 16:7; I Chronicles 28:9; Luke 16:14-15), while man condemns others of acts they themselves are committing (v.1-2). Those committing such acts will not escape the wrath of God (v.3). They spat on God's goodness, not recognizing God's patience for what it was, hardened their *hearts* (ignored their conscience), and laid up for themselves a treasure chest filled with God's wrath (v.5). In His just judgment, God would dump wrath on their sorry souls, but reward those doing good (v.6-9). The Greek and the Jew have equal status because God is no respecter of persons (v.10-11). God will judge the Greek by their conscience (heart) and will judge the Jew according to their performance of the law (v.12-16).

It is important to note in the above scripture that the love of God cannot be separated from the concept of justice (righteousness). The concept of justice (righteousness) always seeks a nexus to consequences. To remove consequences from the life equation is to remove justice (righteousness) via the removal of reward and punishment. To remove consequences from the life equation is to defy the laws of God and His nature. God is love, and God is just. God is love, because he is just. We are confident that if we follow what he has written in our hearts and minds, we will stand justified before Him at the end of our lives. Are we listening to what God has written in our hearts, or are we listening to man's drivel? Are we placing our trust in the *authorities* or God?

In a parallel vein of thought related to the above scripture, how often, as *institutionalized* churchgoers, have we looked at someone outside the church *institution* and commented to ourselves, or others, that so-and-so down the street, or across the way, seems like a really nice person and has a warm and loving spouse and kids who are all well-behaved and respectful of the property of others, but they don't go to church, and oh, wouldn't it be nice if we could just convert them to Christianity (read Churchianity)? We often may have quietly noted that they seemed more like Christians than some of those we had known to be deeply embedded in religious *institutionalism* for years and years. We think this very thought is what Paul is depicting in Romans 2:14-15 where he refers to some Gentiles as performing *naturally* according to the law what others do by rote.

One of the chief distinctions made in the New Testament had to do with the concept of the *spirit of the law* versus the *letter of the law* (II Corinthians 3:3-6). The religious *authorities* of that time were accused by Christ of debating the intricacies (letter) of the law while doing none of it and judging others while guilty of the same acts themselves. They totally missed its spirit. Christ consistently pointed out that we will be judged on the basis of what is contained in our hearts. Not only should we do the right things, but we should do the right things for the right reasons.

If we believe God created the world in six days, is it not possible God placed everything we need to know to attain eternal life in our hearts, as he promised to do? Did not God purposefully do this knowing that *uninspired* and *ungifted* translators would eventually butcher and bastardize His words?

There is no great commission that applies to us today that applied to those in that unique period of spiritual history transiting from the old law to the new law; from the old covenant to the new covenant; and from the old heaven and earth to the new heaven and earth. There is no scriptural authority for the inferior "church club" institutional model led by *uninspired* and *ungifted* men who are appointed or approved by *uninspired* and *ungifted* men in a post A.D. 70 world. There is no scriptural basis for their rules of membership, order of worship, plan of salvation, or missionary work. Divine intervention in the affairs of men ended when God's ultimate mission to restore His sovereign authority was achieved in A.D. 70. No divine healers, exorcists, preachers, pastors, elders, or deacons are operating with scriptural authority in this day and age.

The belief that the rapture and/or second coming of Christ is a *future* event is absent scriptural basis and, therefore, a man-conceived creed. The belief that the rapture and/or second coming of Christ is a past event, however, is scripturally founded and substantiated throughout the entire Bible. We've just touched the tip of the iceberg in comparison to what is available for the reader to explore on his or her own. This exploratory effort should be undertaken with a Greek and Hebrew dictionary available and with the caveat that what is called the Bible is a human and *uninspired* translation. Any study of the Bible without the Greek and Hebrew dictionary available is a personal statement that the reader prefers to place their faith in *uninspired* human translators and prefers to delegate their personal responsibility to human *authority*.

I expect to pass through life but once. If therefore, there be any kindness I can show, or any good thing I can do to any fellow being, let me do it now, and not defer or neglect it, as I shall not pass this way again. – **William Penn**

Chapter 8

The Hijacking of Our Liberty

We've talked about how the *futurist* creed has hijacked our spiritual liberty by promoting an *institutional* church model devoid of *gifted* and *inspired* men with all its inherent rules of conduct, conditional love, unanswered questions, and absence of scriptural authority. Now, we would like to shift our focus to the illicit relationship between the religious *institutions* and the *institution* of civil government and how this unholy alliance seeks to rob us of our physical liberty.

What is the basic underlying core belief held by religious *institutions* serving to legitimize and perpetuate civil government tyranny and oppression over the people? Largely, it is the principle of the divine right of kings.

The divine right of kings principle is a religious and secular belief system that holds to the position that God continues to intervene in the setting up and taking away of kings, or other ruling entities, and that God has ordained those holding these positions of power. The divine right of kings principle, by necessary inference, is the belief that if God didn't want the Hitlers, Stalins, Clintons, and Bushes of the world in power, they wouldn't have been allowed to hold those positions of power. The divine right of kings principle, by necessary inference, is the belief that it was "God's will" that Hitler, Stalin, Clinton, and the Bushes respectively fried, butchered, starved, and slaughtered millions of human beings for equally perverse, diverse, and hideous reasons. In other words, if it hadn't been "God's will," those atrocities would not have taken place.

In applying the divine right of kings logic to the American experiment, things can get interesting in a hurry. The Declaration of Independence basically told King George III to shove off. The Declaration of Independence not only told King George III to shove off, it established as one of its core tenets that all tyrants could shove off, take a hike, go climb a rope, go pound sand, or the like. For those subscribing to the belief that the founding of this nation was based on Christian principles and, by extension, hold to the view the United States is a "Christian nation," this viewpoint presents some serious difficulty. On one hand, Christians allege that "the powers that be" are ordained of God, and we must obey them, while on the other hand, it was somehow ok to not only disobey King George III, but to also violently oppose him. So, which is it? Are we really a Christian nation founded on Christian principles? If so, by what notion was the principle of the divine right of kings abandoned by those Christian colonists advocating the violent overthrow of the king? And by what principle can Christians today celebrate and rejoice in the 4th of July when the basis of that celebration is founded on the violent resisting of "the powers that be?"

There is, of course, the built-in assumption in the above line of questioning that our nation was founded on Christian principles, but we don't necessarily mean to imply this is actually the case. The belief that this nation was founded upon Christian principles, however, is a widely held viewpoint among many Christians and is often used as a basis or justification for the coercive expansion of our empire worldwide. If we are a Christian nation, there is an assumption God is on our side and that we will prevail in any given conflict. This includes the assumption we have a *divine* mandate to aggressively take the battle to those who fail to do our bidding and that preemptive first strikes are an acceptable form of convincing the rest of the world to see things our way.

As a supposedly Christian nation, we are no longer satisfied with ruling over our own affairs, but we must now go outside of our own borders and depose rulers of <u>other</u> countries and then occupy them, just like the British attempted to do here. If it was wrong for the British to lord their rule over the colonies, why is it suddenly ok for the U.S. to depose the rulers of other countries and then occupy and attempt to democratize those countries at great expense of blood, life, energy, property, and morality? If democracy is such a wonderful Christian invention, why do we need a gun to sell it to the rest of the world?

How do we know what God's will is in these matters? Do we only know if it is God's will after the fact, based on who wins a given conflict? If who wins the war is the ultimate determiner of God's will in these matters, we really don't know going into it whether we are opposing God's will or not, do we? After all, Hitler and Stalin must have found some favor with God, or they wouldn't have gotten as far down the killing path as they did, would they? Is it truly a situation where might makes right? If might always makes right, did that make the killing and persecution of God's prophets, apostles, and disciples something honorable?

Do you see the tangled web of convoluted logic that is derived from the *futurist* creed that promotes the concept of the divine right of kings in a post A.D. 70 world?

One key distinction between the territorial battles fought today and the battles depicted in the Bible, conveniently overlooked by many, is that God very visibly intervened in those battles. God spoke to leaders of nations directly. Are there any national leaders today who can claim a similar executive privilege while maintaining a straight face?

In Chapter 4 of this book, we shared the Biblical account of how God's people begged for a king to rule over them and the terrible consequences to befall them for rejecting God's rule and pledging their allegiance and loyalty to a nation and its king or ruler. The people essentially gave up their liberty and became slaves to the State. Some were conscripted into the military or other types of non-volunteer service. Sound familiar? Their property was stolen and given to the king's servants. Doesn't this sound much like the asset forfeiture laws used to fight the war on drugs? People were taxed on their income so the king's servants didn't need to seek productive employment. Their tax was a paltry ten percent, and it was considered outrageous. Here in the United States, combined income, sales, and estate taxes can easily average over 50 percent or more without even considering the hidden tax of inflation, which saps purchasing power while forcing more and more middle-class people into higher tax brackets. Much of the income gains in the last 30 years have only been in nominal terms, with the ongoing debasement of our currency. If a person in 1979 made $20,000 a year and their income grew to $40,000 a year in 2009, they would, in terms of dollar purchasing power and disposable income, have taken a $10,000 pay cut. The $40,000 dollar income places them in a higher tax bracket with less disposable income, and the diminished purchasing power of the dollar erodes their standard of living. They are essentially squeezed from two different directions. In 2009, it would probably take a minimum of $50,000 a year to simply break even with the $20,000 salary earned in 1979. The difference between the two salaries is $30,000, but it represents no actual gain in real income as far as total household goods and services purchased with it. Many people perceive they are making more money, but they are actually losing income in terms of purchasing power. This deception fools the majority of consumers and tricks them into assuming more debt than would normally be considered prudent. The larger paychecks can easily seduce them into feeling euphorically rich and numb them to the point they can never feel and identify the inflation pickpocket lifting their wallets and stealing its contents. They just know it is getting harder and harder to get by and that at the end of the month there is usually more month than money left over.

Tyrants of old clipped the gold and silver coins in circulation to debase the currency and defraud the people. Today's tyrant uses a central bank (Federal Reserve) and a printing press to defraud the people along with the minting of clad coins whereby cheaper base metals have been substituted for precious metals (gold and silver). This pattern of theft has been relatively unchanged throughout history, with the only noted differences being the methodology. Technology has made the process of governmental theft a bit more obscure and has allowed the attention of the people to be diverted away from the real culprits by the resultant social conflict that always arises when unjust weights and measures becomes *institutionalized*.

Our fraudulent fractional reserve banking system has been the direct source of some of the most severe financial calamities this nation has had to endure. When price inflation eventually rears its ugly head, few people will look at the true source of the ugliness (a fraudulent banking system) but will, instead, protest the high prices and demand that price controls be instituted. The political pressure associated with civil unrest will bring on price controls. Price controls kill profit potential and place businesses in bankruptcy or they become nationalized. This leads to scarcity, rationing, and even more civil unrest. People blindly turn to government to be rescued from each and every subsequent crisis, with few taking the time to consider that government was responsible for causing the original crisis that spawned all the rest. Many people continue to buy the two biggest lies that have been with us since the beginning of time. Those lies are (1) we can have something for nothing and (2) there are no consequences for ignoring truth and/or the acceptance of lies.

Liberty isn't taken, stolen, or lost, as much as it is simply given up by those who don't value it. Many people willingly trade the truth for a lie and suffer the consequences each and every time.

Earlier we mentioned the Biblical account of how God's people begged for a king (a man) to rule over them and the terrible consequences to befall them for rejecting God's rule and pledging, instead, their allegiance and loyalty to a nation and its king or ruler. Speaking to the issue of the pledge of allegiance, we have a question. If the "powers that be," or kings, are divinely ordained by God, wouldn't that place <u>all</u> nations under God? If all nations are truly under God, couldn't we say the pledge of allegiance to all nations? In light of this, what significance does the pledge of allegiance really have? And by what superior and inequality promoting mindset can we place a bumper sticker on our car that states, God bless America? If all nations are under God (ordained), wouldn't a more Christian attitude be reflected with a bumper sticker stating, God bless <u>all</u> nations? Also, by what superior and inequality promoting mindset can we place a bumper sticker on our car that reads, God bless our troops? If all nations are under God (ordained), wouldn't a more Christian attitude be reflected with a bumper sticker reading, God bless their troops also? Do some of us really believe that God is an American?

> *It was a time of great and exalting excitement. The country was up in arms, the war was on, in every breast burned the holy fire*

of patriotism; the drums were beating, the bands playing, the toy pistols popping, the bunched firecrackers hissing and sputtering; on every hand and far down the receding and fading spreads of roofs and balconies a fluttering wilderness of flags flashed in the sun; daily the young volunteers marched down the wide avenue gay and fine in their new uniforms, the proud fathers and mothers and sisters and sweethearts cheering them with voices choked with happy emotion as they swung by; nightly the packed mass meetings listened, panting, to patriot oratory which stirred the deepest deeps of their hearts and which they interrupted at briefest intervals with cyclones of applause, the tears running down their cheeks the while; in the churches the pastors preached devotion to flag and country and invoked the God of Battles, beseeching His aid in our good cause in outpouring of fervid eloquence which moved every listener.

It was indeed a glad and gracious time, and the half dozen rash spirits that ventured to disapprove of the war and cast a doubt upon its righteousness straightway got such a stern and angry warning that for their personal safety's sake they quickly shrank out of sight and offended no more in that way.

Sunday morning came – next day the battalions would leave for the front; the church was filled; the volunteers were there, their faces alight with material dreams – visions of a stern advance, the gathering momentum, the rushing charge, the flashing sabers, the flight of the foe, the tumult, the enveloping smoke, the fierce pursuit, the surrender! – then home from the war, bronzed heros, welcomed, adored, submerged in golden seas of glory! With the volunteers sat their dear ones, proud, happy, and envied by the neighbors and friends who had no sons and brothers to send forth to the field of honor, there to win for the flag or, failing, die the noblest of noble deaths. The service proceeded; a war chapter from the Old Testament was read; the first prayer was said; it was followed by an organ burst that shook the building, and with one impulse the house rose, with glowing eyes and beating hearts, and poured out that tremendous invocation – "God the all-terrible! Thou who ordainest, Thunder thy clarion and lightning thy sword!"

Then came the "long" prayer. None could remember the like of it for passionate pleading and moving and beautiful language. The burden of its supplication was that an ever-merciful and benignant Father of us all would watch over our noble young soldiers and aid, comfort, and encourage them in their patriotic work; bless them, shield them in His mighty hand, make them strong and confident, invincible in the bloody onset; help them to crush the foe, grant to them and to their flag and country imperishable honor and glory.

An aged stranger entered and moved with slow and noiseless step up the main aisle, his eyes fixed upon the minister, his long body clothed in a robe that reached to his feet, his head bare, his white hair descending in a frothy cataract to his shoulders, his seamy face unnaturally pale, pale even to ghastliness. With all eyes following him and wondering, he made his silent way; without pausing, he ascended to the preacher's side and stood there, waiting.

With shut lids the preacher, unconscious of his presence, continued his moving prayer, and at last finished it with the words, uttered in fervent appeal," Bless our arms, grant us the victory, O Lord our God, Father and Protector of our land and flag!"

The stranger touched his arm, motioned him to step aside – which the startled minister did – and took his place. During some moments he surveyed the spellbound audience with solemn eyes in which burned an uncanny light; then in a deep voice he said

"I come from the Throne – bearing a message from Almighty God!" The words smote the house with a shock; if the stranger perceived it he gave no attention. "He has heard the prayer of His servant your shepherd and grant it if such shall be your desire after I, His messenger, shall have explained to you its import – that is to say, its full import. For it is like unto many of the prayers of men, in that it asks for more than he who utters it is aware of – except he pause and think.

"God's servant and yours has prayed his prayer. Has he paused and taken thought? Is it one prayer? No, it is two – one uttered, the other not. Both have reached the ear of His Who hearth all

supplications, the spoken and the unspoken. Ponder this – keep it in mind. If you beseech a blessing upon yourself, beware! lest without intent you invoke a curse upon a neighbor at the same time. If you pray for the blessing of rain upon your crop which needs it, by that act you are possibly praying for a curse upon some neighbor's crop which may not need rain and can be injured by it.

"You have heard your servant's prayer – the uttered part of it. I am commissioned by God to put into words the other part of it – that part which the pastor, and also you in your hearts, fervently prayed silently. And ignorantly and unthinkingly? God grant that it was so! You heard these words: 'Grant us the victory, O Lord our God!' That is sufficient. The whole of the uttered prayer is compact into those pregnant words. Elaborations were not necessary. When you have prayed for victory you have prayed for many unmentioned results which follow victory – must follow it, cannot help but follow it. Upon the listening spirit of God the Father fell also the unspoken part of the prayer. He commandeth me to put it into words. Listen!

"O Lord our Father, our young patriots, idols of our hearts, go forth to battle – be Thou near them! With them, in spirit, we also go forth from the sweet peace of our beloved firesides to smite the foe. O Lord our God, help us to tear their soldiers to bloody shreds with our shells; help us to cover their smiling fields with the pale forms of their patriot dead; help us to drown the thunder of the guns with the shrieks of their wounded, writhing in pain; help us to lay waste their humble homes with a hurricane of fire; help us to wring the hearts of their unoffending widows with unavailing grief; help us to turn them out roofless with their little children to wander unfriended the wastes of their desolated land in rags and hunger and thirst, sports of the sun flames of summer and the icy winds of winter, broken in spirit, worn with travail, imploring Thee for the refuge of the grave and denied it – for our sakes who adore Thee, Lord, blast their hopes, blight their lives, protract their bitter pilgrimage, make heavy their steps, water their way with their tears, stain the white snow with the blood of their wounded feet! We ask it, in the spirit of love, of Him Who is the Source of Love, and Who is ever-faithful *refuge and friend of all that are sore beset and seek His aid with humble and contrite hearts. Amen.*

(After a pause)

"Ye have prayed it; if ye still desire it, speak! The messenger of the Most High waits."

It was believed afterward that the man was a lunatic, because there was no sense in what he said. – **Mark Twain, The War Prayer**

If the nature of nations is transitory (a cyclical rising and falling), and if God, from time to time, can turn His back to a wicked nation, or vice versa, wouldn't it be possible that a Christian could be pledging his earthly allegiance and loyalty to something inherently wicked and evil?

Consider for a moment how big of a hot button issue the pledge of allegiance is in public schools to the Christian community. They often turn their children's young minds over to government-controlled indoctrination centers to have their minds molded and shaped after the image of Ba'al and then are affronted over the pledge of allegiance because it didn't include the phrase "one nation under God." Equally disturbing is how many in the Christian community are offended over the fact their child can't pray in these government-run indoctrination centers. What are they doing sending their children there in the first place? The debate should not be about how the pledge, prayer, or homosexuality is packaged in public schools, but rather whether we should have government involved with education at all. If government (and our tax dollars) was removed from the education equation, the less important hot button issues of how the pledge, prayer, and homosexuality are packaged would die a quite natural and fitting death. Those tax dollars could be returned to the taxpayer, where they would be free to choose the education venue most appropriate to their belief system, thereby increasing their personal liberty while, at the same time, decreasing the intrusion of government in their lives. The only people who would be offended with this type of arrangement would be those who believe themselves to be superior and thereby entitled to force their viewpoint onto others.

Liberty-loving people are not waiting for the masses to jump on board with them in the area of educating their children. While they may not all be in a position to withdraw their tax dollars from a failed public education system, many are withdrawing their children from public schools and teaching them at home or finding suitable private education for their children. Those families teaching their children at home have often chosen a reduced standard of living with only one parent being the breadwinner while the other parent tends to the needs of the home and the education of their children. In doing so, they've often reduced their incomes and, by necessity, their consumption. The additional benefit of this approach is their support to a government that is no longer promoting liberty is being reduced, while their children are being taught the difference between satisfying needs versus wants. Generally, what we truly need is provided in abundance if we don't first become distracted with the non-essentials and lose our focus. During the next decade or so of financial change and upheaval, a moving away from an overly consumptive lifestyle to one of thrift may prove to be a very valuable legacy to impart to one's children.

Does it not often appear a goal of the public education system is to dumb down the populace to more easily control and assimilate them into a centrally planned and managed society? The more curious, passionate, and energetic children, not easily corralled or channeled into this indoctrination program, are given chemical lobotomies after being diagnosed by educators as being restless, hyperactive, or having short attention spans.

The irony is that educators who sponsor D.A.R.E. presentations in student assemblies and classrooms to teach kids about the evils and dangers of drugs and drug abuse are acting as enablers to a much larger and more insidious drug distribution network whereby ritalin, commonly referred to as kiddie cocaine, is being dispensed and abused widely. Some have tied the student use of ritalin and other such drugs with school shootings across the country. The focus of attention, in these instances, is usually drawn to the availability of firearms while ignoring the availability of drugs and the blatant distribution being facilitated and promoted by educators in the public school system.

While the police are guarding the front doors of these educational *institutions* in an attempt to provide early interdiction efforts, the educators are playing the part of mules who've been duped into trafficking corporate dope in through the back door. And quite unlike shady underworld pharmacists, who are lurking in the shadows and on the dodge from the police, these corporate *upper*world pharmacists actually have the protection of the police and use the coercive arm of the state to force potentially harmful and mind-altering drugs on children without parental consent. In some cases, if it appears the parents may object to the shanghaiing of their kids into the corporate *upper*world program of mental sterilization, the children are forcibly removed from the home and placed in *institutions* where only supervised contact is allowed between parent and child. We've heard that schools receive a proportional amount of budgetary funding directly related to the number of students who are enrolled in this mental sterilization program. The overprescribing of these drugs has become so prolific in many schools that there is a student black market for surplus prescriptions, leading to dependency and addictions that would otherwise not have happened. All of this, of course, is happening under the watchful eyes of the establishment *authorities* who are purportedly acting in the child's best interest.

Under a flawed system of political law, as we've stated previously, it is not <u>what</u> is done (establishment of pharmacies and drug distribution networks), but <u>who</u> done it that most often distinguishes the law breakers from the law abiding. In a society that respects liberty, equality, and justice, the act in question is either illegal for all or illegal for none. If a given act is prohibited for the individual to do, it is also prohibited for the *collective* to do. The *collective* (society) is only a multiple of the individual. A multiple or majority of participants committing a given act should not be the measuring stick used to determine the legal or moral supremacy of that act in those societies claiming to respect and promote liberty.

Why do many people consistently choose the phony over the real deal? Because they believe the lies that they can have something for nothing and that there are no consequences for ignoring truth. We have fiat money, fiat food and drugs, fiat religion, fiat government, fiat education, and fiat healthcare. Fiat anything is simply a speaking or writing of something into officially sanctioned existence. It is a rubber stamping process denoting official approval, as in USDA approved, or some type of licensure. Fiat anything may resemble something tangible and real, but it is usually lacking a core and essential ingredient from that which it is attempting to imitate. It exists significantly by decree, rather than substance. It is the vain attempt by man of speaking something into existence in much the same way God spoke the world into existence. We have money by government decree (debased), food by government decree (debased and unnaturally packaged), religion by government decree [(501(c)(3)], government by decree (executive orders), education by government decree (licensure), and healthcare by government decree (licensure). The perpetrators are, in effect, pretending to be gods, and their worshippers bow down before these false gods when they accept these decrees as representing something real and true. We have banking and treasury czars, education czars, food and drug czars, religion czars, healthcare czars, and presidential czars ruling by executive order, or even martial law, when the Constitution becomes an annoyance. These czars give their stamp of approval for these inferior imitations of <u>the real deal</u>, and by simple decree they become approved, but they come into existence as something far removed from a more natural and superior version the marketplace could provide if government would only get out of the way and quit interfering. When people place their faith in government czars to protect them, they abdicate their personal responsibility and reap the consequences, as we now witness on an almost daily basis.

Many people in our society would turn up their noses and walk quickly past a stainless steel bucket full of fresh and natural cow's milk for the preference of purchasing an expensive and inferior imitation in the grocery store. If the fiat version (government approved) stagnates in their stomach undigested and they develop various allergies, do they question this anomaly or just accept what the *authorities* have to say about it?

Many people in our society would quite willingly walk past a pure one ounce gold or silver coin (just weights and measures), often touted as a barbaric relic of the past, for the preference of acquiring pieces of fiat paper with ink images of dead guys printed on them representing a pseudo monetary product (*unjust* weights and measures) of a supposedly more enlightened and intellectual society. When the fiat currency fails, like every fiat currency has in the past, do people question it or just accept the pronouncements of the *authorities*?

Many people in our society would quite willingly walk past a private school for the preference of a free public education that consistently fails to deliver on its promise to win the war on illiteracy. Isn't it obvious how the gullible public has been snookered by the big lie that they can have something for nothing and that there are no consequences for ignoring truth? Illiteracy is climbing exponentially in this country.

The war on illiteracy, if it continues to be waged in the public sector, will have much in common with the war on drugs, the war on poverty, and the war on terror in that they all have become known as the "forever" wars. The financial incentives associated with the continuance of these "forever" wars significantly outweigh the incentive for winning them. The ever-expanding bureaucracies created to prosecute these wars have a rather glaring conflict of interest inherent in their structures. If they accomplish their mission statement, their cushy gigs are up. So, what do you think the likelihood is for that happening?

Why does a supposedly Christian nation put up with all of this foolish nonsense when it is glaringly false, liberty-limiting, dream-killing, inequality promoting, and unjust? This nonsense continues because of the belief in the divine right of kings. They believe God is in charge and that they don't have to accept responsibility for their ill-conceived beliefs and subsequent choices. They believe it is God's will that humanity races each other to the bottom of the morality barrel. Religious *institutions* promote this flawed belief to their congregants, and tyrants grinningly accept the *divine* calling pronounced upon them by their spiritual counterparts. Religious *institutions* have their own form of internal government patterned more after that of their secular counterparts than any *divine* example found in scripture. Their *institutional* goals and aspirations are as mutually supportive today as they were in early New Testament times when the profane Jewish religious leaders co-opted (as in sold out) with the Romans to oppress and tyrannize the people.

We've discovered that the <u>greater</u> the number of *institutional* intermediaries we've come to rely on in the areas of religion, education, healthcare, food, and finance, the more potential there is for an inordinate and undeserved amount of power to be centralized in the hands of a few, to our own detriment and loss of personal liberty. Conversely, the <u>less</u> we rely on *institutional* intermediaries in the areas of religion, education, healthcare, food, and finance, power is effectively decentralized (middlemen removed) and transferred away from the *institution,* with the resultant benefit of increased personal liberty and enhanced quality of life. This is not to say it is improper to delegate personal responsibility for outcomes to others, but rather that it is probably time we reevaluate those key relationships and determine if those we've delegated such power to are actually worthy of it. In other words, if those we delegate power to don't share our underlying core values, we will most likely be disappointed with a less-than-harmonious outcome. Technical competency combined with shared fundamental core values will usually give the best result.

It has been our observation *institutions*, as part of their self-preservation mechanism, have the most to gain from dividing, labeling, and creating conflict between competing social classes. It is rarely, if ever, the *institution* itself is ever questioned as being the originator and source of the conflict. It is rarely, if ever, the *institution* itself is questioned as to its failed promises of protection. If there is a point of failure somewhere along the way, the only questions the *institutional* high priests allow into the discussion is by how much and by what method *institutional* power may be expanded. The dissolution of the *institution* is never up for discussion. The boundaries of discussion always remain within the confines of the *institution*. What usually escapes the masses during periods of *institutional* upheaval, as we are currently witnessing in the financial markets, where power is being rapidly expanded, is there can never be an expansion of *institutional* power without a corresponding and equal decrease in personal liberty. Fear, therefore, becomes the tool tyrants and *authoritarians* use to expand their power and control over the people.

Political debates are most often limited to the hot button issues of prayer in public schools, the pledge of allegiance, sex education, and homosexuality. These hot button issues excite and arouse the emotions of both liberals and conservatives but obscure a much more important issue. The political debate should be centered on the subject of autonomous freewill, with the only role of government being the protection of individual liberty within the context of the golden rule.

When we successfully force our morality onto others, we have to accept the inevitable reality that what goes around, comes around. If we live by the sword, we will die by the sword. If we value our own liberty, we must value the liberty of all, even if we disagree with their lifestyle or choices. If God granted each one of us liberty or autonomous freewill, by what right or authority does anyone have in attempting to abolish it through coercive (political, legislative) means? How can we attack the liberty of others without realizing we are undermining our own liberty at the same time?

If we closely examine the concept of legislating morality, we find that it is deeply rooted in the Puritan mindset. Puritans feel compelled to proclaim the truth (the gospel) unto the world and convert the heathen from their sinful ways. The implied notion inherent, in this not so humble mindset, is that those who have the truth are to a degree superior (whether as holders of the truth or simply forgiven) to those who haven't yet reached that spiritual pinnacle, or spiritual plane, thereby justifying the use of coercion, via the political and legislative process. What they've failed to realize is that God doesn't want our forced loyalty, but rather He desires our loyalty as freely given and from the heart.

We've not encountered any New Testament examples where coercion was an approved method of evangelizing. Matter of fact, when Christ came upon the adulterous woman about to be stoned by some local Puritans, he put a sudden stop to the process by saying, "He who is without sin cast the first stone." There is a message in that story that gets lost on many who believe they are responsible for the behavior of others.

Let's suppose for a moment the religious *institutions* had an awakening and suddenly recognized the *futurist* position was flawed and that divine intervention associated with the setting up of kings and taking them away was a phenomenon of a bygone era, before A.D. 70. Additionally, they honestly recognize their own religious *institutions* are only a *partial* and grossly inadequate imitation of a congregational model, associated with a bygone era, and the tabernacle of God is now residing with each individual (Revelation 21:3) rather than with *institutions*. Suddenly, they see the decentralization of spiritual *authority* (removal of middlemen) not only in the religious *institutional* realm, but begin also to transfer the same concept to the secular realm of civil *authority*.

If Christians everywhere suddenly realized they could withdraw their consent to obey the powers that be and felt no unnecessary guilt, how would that limit the power of a tyrannical and out-of-control government? How much freer would a person feel if they didn't feel beholden to a bully government? Would the action of civil disobedience by Christians be anarchy? When you have an out-of-control government body that consistently rewards those who do evil while punishing those who do good and while disregarding the rule of law, who are the <u>real</u> anarchists or law breakers? If someone loves God with all their heart, mind, and soul, and loves their neighbor as themselves, by what perverse standard of conduct could they be considered outlaws or anarchists simply because they withdrew their consent to be pillaged and plundered for the purpose of strengthening their oppressor?

What if the religious masses quietly disengaged from practicing *authority* worship in both the religious <u>and</u> secular *institutional* realm? Can you begin to see the implications for liberty with this type of awakening? With our current system of government, we already have anarchy! By returning to the natural law of loving our neighbors as ourselves, or practicing the golden rule, we become law abiding. The practice of the golden rule would eliminate many of the conflicts we encounter today. Our man-conceived and inferior system of political law has severely perverted the concept of justice and equality.

We are not so naïve in our thinking that we believe no one will intentionally take advantage of their neighbor under these circumstances, and some will unwittingly invite their own victimization by falsely believing unconditional love and unconditional trust to be one and the same thing. Our Creator is certainly deserving of our unconditional trust, but man isn't. If we give our trust unconditionally to others, we simply become dupes for every snake-oil salesman and con artist who comes along. We may often consciously choose to overlook unintentional and occasional encroachments, in recognition of our own imperfections, but we should become astute in recognizing when someone else's interests and our own best interests diverge and be willing to take swift action to protect ourselves in such situations.

Such a collective change in attitudes will certainly not happen overnight, but we don't feel we have to wait until everyone gets on board with the concept to enjoy the benefits. Simply withdrawing our faith and reverence for establishment *authority* and accepting personal responsibility for our own outcomes can spare us from much of the *institutional* mischief and calamity thrust on people who've been duped into believing the *authorities* are watching out for their interests. Quite frankly, the *authorities* are usually too busy watching out for their own interests to be concerned with ours.

Owners of capital will stimulate the working class to buy more and more expensive goods, houses and technology, pushing them to take on more and more expensive debt, until their debt becomes unbearable. The unpaid debt will lead to the bankruptcy of all banks, which will have to be nationalized, and the State will have to take the road which will eventually lead to communism." - **Karl Marx, *Das Kapital***

~

In Conclusion

We've received tremendous personal benefit from writing this book. It has allowed us to organize our thoughts, validate our premises, discard some of our flawed beliefs, and fast forward our own personal growth in our continuing quest to harmonize our lives with the laws of nature and nature's God. It has changed our lives.

Love is a natural law no different than the law of gravity. We violate either at great risk to our physical and spiritual well-being. According to I John 3:14, love is the bridge that takes us from our human *fleshly* existence into the eternal spirit world. For ourselves, now that we know love is <u>it</u>, and we don't have to preach it, teach it, or judge it…we can get on with this new experience of simply living it and striving to let God's love be reflected in all our actions. Personally, we are finding the experience somewhat awkward and, at times, very challenging. This is a new experience for us as our previously learned *institutional* behavior of exclusivity (<u>my</u> church is better than <u>your</u> church) darkened our reflective surface to such an extent it was difficult to lovingly accept others unconditionally, as Christ did for us, out of fear of compromising our creed or doctrine.

Some may declare, "Wait a minute. You tell us we don't need to preach in a post A.D. 70 world, but if that's the case, aren't you preaching to us with this book?" In our view, there is a big difference between sharing information on a take it or leave it basis, as we've done, versus the *institutional* message of authority worship. If we were to publish a map someone could take with them to use on a trip, would that be preaching? If we published a book of recipes, would that be preaching? If we shared information about a natural law, such as the law of gravity, would that be preaching? No, preaching denotes *human* spiritual authority. A preacher, by necessary inference, says to his audience, "I have the truth, and I'm imparting it to you." Institutional preachers, elders, and deacons are very quick to warn their *flocks* that if they leave the safety of the *institutional* confines, they are effectively turning their back on God and face eternal damnation. Nowhere in this book have we advocated *human* spiritual authority or *institutional* authority in a post A.D. 70 world.

Institutions, often conceived in good intentions, have a well-documented history for eventually placing *institutional* goals above the needs and well-being of individuals. Rather than the *institutions* remaining servants to the people, the people become servants to the *institutions,* and a form of slavery emerges. There is no love in slavery. *Institutions* have a great propensity for breeding hate, discord, and social class warfare while throwing the world out of sync with natural law. This pattern exists in both the secular and religious *institutional* realm. That very fact is the reason God dispensed with *institutional* authority in A.D. 70 for those accepting citizenship in His spiritual kingdom. *Institutional* authority was conceived in sin and represented a pseudo replacement for God.

In our growing up years, while attending church services, we heard and read about the Biblical accounts of adultery and fornication and thought it had to do primarily with the human *fleshly* act. We've learned since, however, that most Biblical references regarding adultery and fornication are a depiction of spiritual adultery and fornication wherein the people sought to be ruled by men and *institutions* of men, instead of their Creator. Sodom and Gomorrah were cities certainly representative of *fleshly* evils and were destroyed most thoroughly for their evil, but they came in a distant second place to the *spiritual* evil and wickedness taking place in the Judaic world and kindled God's wrath in a much more severe manner during the destruction of Jerusalem, which was known spiritually as Sodom (Revelation 11:8; Matthew 10:15). Jerusalem was the center of the Judaic world and the place where Christ was crucified.

The *my church is better than your church* institutional creed flag waving is somewhat akin to the antics of nationalistic and patriotic flag waving at Olympic sports events or the pennant waving at a high school glee club event. Eventually and quite tragically, these seemingly innocent antics are often the breeding ground for flag waving of a more serious and intense nature where the lives of innocent men, women, and children actually hang in the balance at the whim of an egoistic and greedy military-industrial complex bent on saving the world by preemptive and indiscriminate killing.

We now find ourselves, nationally speaking, speculating about who our future enemies *could* be and targeting them for preemptive murder while calling it self-defense. This outrage would be analogous to speculating about our neighbor across the street who we observed looking at us crossways and making a determination that we must kill him <u>now</u> before he *might* kill us later. And while we are at it, we might as well kill his wife and kids also, because they will probably hold a grudge against us that could impact us or our own children later.

There are so-called Christians warming pews all across this nation who have given a silent wink and a nod to this murderous outrage while totally ignoring what is in their heart as they cling ever so tightly to Romans 13:1-7. Most Christians would probably be surprised to know there are 14 verses in Romans chapter 13 and would be equally shocked to know what those last seven verses espouse. Why they seem to take a crusader's solace in the first seven verses while ignoring the last seven is beyond our capacity to rationalize. What they've obviously failed to take into consideration is that the need for God to directly intervene in the affairs of man is no longer necessary. His promises to provide a Savior and restore His sovereign authority were fulfilled in A.D. 70. Throughout Old Testament history, and to include the A.D. 70 time frame, God used the kingdoms of men, under Satan's dominion, to protect the linage of Christ and ultimately ensure His promises were fulfilled. He used the Roman government to punish the evil Jewish religious *authorities* and their followers in Jerusalem, and also for the purpose of destroying the tabernacle and Jerusalem in A.D 70. The purpose of Romans 13 (read the entire chapter and chapter 12 also) was to simply let Christians know that they were not to interfere or intervene. God was in charge of the events about to transpire, the time was short, and they needed to keep their eye on the ball. In other words, they were being admonished to <u>not</u> get entangled with government by resisting it out of some misplaced allegiance and unearned loyalty to their evil and profane Jewish religious leaders and *authorities* who had perverted the law and were responsible for killing the prophets, murdering Christ, tormenting His disciples, and were about to be pounced upon by *outsiders*.

We see this concept very clearly in the Muslim world. Various Muslim sects fight among themselves with great tenacity and fierceness, but they will immediately cease and desist in their warring with one another to pull together and join forces against any *outsiders* attempting to invade and occupy their shared territories.

So the message of Paul was clear. Stay out of the impending conflict and continue abiding in Christ because the *outsiders* (the Romans) were going to give the profane Jewish religious *authorities* exactly as they deserved and as God had promised. He was not implying that government be revered. Quite the contrary, the context of these passages represented an advisory to them to avoid the God-directed mushroom cloud that was going to be enveloping and destroying the errant Jewish religious world as they knew it. Time was short, there was still work to be done, and they needed to keep focused.

The *futurists* are caught in a time warp. They are trapped and incarcerated in a prison of their own maintaining and from which there is no escape until they discard their man-conceived creed. This evil and man-conceived *futurist* creed butchers and bastardizes scripture like no other man-conceived creed has ever done before. Christ came to open the prison doors, and this creed, to those who buy into it, effectively slams the prison doors shut again with a deafening clang. Interestingly, these prison doors appear to be locked, but they are not. All that is necessary to begin the process of regaining the liberty Christ so freely gave all of us is to simply question man-conceived authority. Once this is done, the prison doors will again swing open, and the light of the truth will enter *naturally* and remove the darkness. How does this happen? When we begin to question man's *authority* we, by necessity, become more personally responsible for our own outcomes and one-by-one begin discarding those inhibiting beliefs that we can't validate with our own innate reasoning ability. Instead of marching to the beat of someone else's drum, we begin to allow ourselves the opportunity and privilege of marching to the beat of our own inner drum. We begin paying more attention to that inner voice we've so often ignored in the past. How many times have we said, "I should have listened to my heart"? We can either choose to trust our own heart, or the heart of someone else. But before making this vitally important choice we must first ask ourselves an important question. That question is, "Who truly has the greatest interest in our own personal well-being?" Who ultimately bears the brunt of the choices we make? Isn't it about time we learn to listen to what our own hearts are telling us instead of those self-appointed gurus who claim to have our best interests at heart?

If the reader hasn't gained any other benefit from reading this work other than continuing to entertain the *possibility* of the rapture being a <u>past</u> event, they will never read the Bible the same again; because if a person can entertain the *possibility* of the rapture being a <u>past</u> event, they by necessity, must also entertain the *possibility* of the Bible being a book of <u>history</u> rather than a book containing unfulfilled prophecy.

Each and every time the Bible is read, with this new level of understanding, it offers the reader a tremendously rewarding and liberating experience. But it will be a rather sickening and empty experience for those readers who've chosen to unquestioningly accept the man-conceived filter (creed) handed to them by the *authorities* with all its inherent flaws and unanswered questions.

A tyrant must put on the appearance of uncommon devotion to religion. Subjects are less apprehensive of illegal treatment from a ruler whom they consider god-fearing and pious. **- Aristotle**

INDEX

4th of July, 91
A.D. 70, 31, 32, 33, 35, 39, 54, 56, 64, 67, 68, 76, 77, 80, 88, 89, 92, 107, 110, 111, 113
abomination of desolation, 47
absence of lies, 15, 22
accident of birth, 13
all nations under God, 95
allegiance, 3, 82, 83, 85, 93, 95, 99, 106, 113
anarchy, 107, 108
antichrists, 45, 66
Aristotle, 28, 29, 115
asset forfeiture laws, 93
automatons, 4, 27
availability of drugs, 101
Babel, 61
bad food and drugs, 5
ball and chain, 10
bank run of 1929, 20
Barrow, Alaska, 17
belief system, 10, 12, 13, 23, 25, 34, 79, 90
biases, 3, 29, 33, 38
Bible, 30, 32, 33, 34, 37, 38, 39, 46, 47, 49, 50, 52, 54, 58, 75, 81, 89, 92, 115
Bible translations, 39
bit and bridle, 10
blind faith, 4
bondage, 6, 7, 34, 40, 41, 51, 65, 79, 84
Bushes, 90
Catholic church, 11, 35
chemical lobotomies, 100
chicken in every pot, 20
children, 32, 46, 47, 57, 65, 73, 77, 82, 84, 98, 99, 100, 101, 112
Chinese Proverb, 14
Christian nation, 91, 92, 104
Christians, 6, 17, 18, 31, 32, 34, 62, 75, 81, 88, 91, 107, 112, 113
church and state, 6
church club, 78, 81, 88
church of Christ, 3
Churchianity, 88
civil government, 6, 90
civil unrest, 6, 94
Civil War, 10, 81
Clinton, 90
coercion, 7, 17, 82, 106, 107
coming in the clouds, 46, 48
con artist, 108
conditional love, 90, 108
conscience, 65, 84, 86, 87
consequences, 2, 29, 41, 65, 87, 93, 95, 102, 103, 104
Constitution, 103
contingent beliefs, 22
corporate *upper*world pharmacists, 101
Creator, 3, 4, 7, 13, 108, 111
creed, 4, 29, 30, 31, 33, 34, 35, 46, 47, 51, 83, 89, 90, 92, 110, 112, 114, 115
crucifying Christ, 35
czars, 103
D.A.R.E., 101
Dark Age, 28
Das Kapital, 109
decentralized, 44, 105
Declaration of Independence, 91
denominations, 30
divine intervention, 5, 78, 88, 107
divine right of kings, 3, 5, 28, 39, 40, 90, 91, 92, 104
doctrinal differences, 30
drug abuse, 101
due diligence, 24, 25
Ecuador, 16, 17
elephant, 16, 33
enslaved, 40
enslaves, 84
equality, 2, 79, 102, 108
Eskimo, 17
Etienne De La Boetie, 26
exploitation, 2, 35
Federal Reserve, 21, 94
fiat education, 102
fiat food and drugs, 102
fiat government, 102
fiat healthcare, 102
fiat money, 102

fiat religion, 102
financial bailout, 2
financial fraudsters, 5
fish wrap, 12
flags and crosses, 6
flat earth dogmas, 17
flesh brokers, 79
forever wars, 104
fractional reserve banking system, 21, 94
fraud, 7, 19, 21, 31, 79
fraudulent financial practices, 21
freewill, 2, 4, 63, 106
fried, butchered, starved and slaughtered, 90
Galileo Galilei, 41
Garden of Eden, 41, 42, 61
God bless America, 95
God bless our troops, 95
God is an American?, 95
God is in charge, 104
God is in control, 5
God is just, 87
God is love, 73, 87
God is on our side, 91
God's authority, 35, 40, 41, 61
God's will, 90, 91, 92, 104
golden rule, 2, 17, 106, 108
government, 99, 100, 102, 103, 104, 106, 107, 108, 113
great commission, 55, 68, 85, 88
great sound of a trumpet, 46, 48
hedge fund manager, 20, 21
hidden tax of inflation, 93
higher tax brackets, 93
Hitler, 90, 92
human experience, 79
hypocrites, 18, 82
illiteracy, 5, 104
indoctrination centers, 99
inequality, 3, 95, 104
inflation pickpocket, 94
inherited beliefs, 31
inherited viewpoint, 29
innocent eyes, 84
inspired word of God, 33, 37, 38, 39, 54, 58, 77, 81
institutional group think, 36
institutional hamster wheel, 83
intellectual decapitation, 1

intermediaries, 24, 104, 105
Internet, 11, 12
jackasses, 21
Judaic Age, 35, 42, 45, 57, 60, 66, 75, 76
justice, 66, 67, 79, 86, 87, 102, 108
Karl Marx, 109
kiddie cocaine, 101
King George III, 91
kingdom of Nimrod, 61
kingdoms of men, 35, 38, 39, 40, 41, 51, 63, 64, 65, 79, 113
landscape of our minds, 9
last days prophecy, 34
law of gravity, 18, 19, 110, 111
Law of Moses, 57
laws of nature, 2, 3, 110
letter of the law, 88
libertarian, 6, 7, 17
liberty, 1
lies and truth, 15
love thy neighbor as thyself, 85
Mark Twain, 99
mental sterilization, 101
might makes right, 92
millennialism, 34
Nanny State, 35, 40, 82
natural law, 2, 3, 5, 108, 110, 111
no free lunch, 20
non-denominations, 30
obedience, 4, 26, 84, 85, 107
obeying the powers that be, 6
one nation under God, 99
Pavlov's dogs, 9
pledge of allegiance, 95, 99, 106
political law, 2, 102, 108
Pope, 35, 38
pounding the pulpit, 75
poverty, 5, 104
preachers, 23, 36, 66, 74, 89, 111
preemptively killing, 31
price controls, 94
price inflation, 94
printing press, 11, 38, 94
prison, 1, 26, 27, 42, 114
private school, 103
promotion of war and genocide, 34
proprietary interest, 24
public education system, 100
public schools, 11, 99, 100, 106

Puritan mindset, 106
reformation, restitution, and *refreshing*, 35
Republican Party, 12
ritalin, 101
Roman government, 113
Romans 13, 52, 85, 112, 113
Ron Paul, 11, 12
Savings and Loan debacle of the 1980s, 20
school shootings, 101
scorpions, 55, 56
second coming, 33, 34, 44, 45, 46, 47, 48, 54, 56, 58, 60, 61, 66, 70, 75, 76, 77, 83, 89
shady underworld pharmacists, 101
slave, 10, 13, 93
slavery, 10, 111
snake-oil salesmen, 5, 108
social conflict, 94
Social Security Ponzi scheme, 20, 21
something for nothing, 20, 95, 102, 104
sound of a trumpet, 46, 48
sovereignty, 5, 11, 42, 66, 77, 78, 86
speak to them smooth things, 65
spirit of the law, 88
spiritual beings, 43, 79
spiritual Sodom, 60, 61, 67
spiritual survival, 11
Stalin, 90, 92
support of the state of Israel, 34
tabernacle missing in action, 76
Ten Commandments, 85, 86
terrorists, 5
The Politics of Obedience; The Discourse of Voluntary Servitude **circa 1552**, 26
the powers that be, 6, 91, 107
The War Prayer, 99
Thomas Jefferson, 7, 82
time warp, 114
tribulation, 46, 48, 59
two biggest lies, 95
tyranny, 7, 25, 40, 41, 79, 90
tyrants, 11, 91, 94, 104, 106
unconditional love, 108
unconditional trust, 108
unjust weights and measures, 94, 103
unmitigated arrogance, 18
war bandwagon, 17
war on drugs, 93, 104
war on illiteracy, 104

war on poverty, 104
war on terror, 104
William Penn, 89
withdrawing our consent, 25